D1711214

LAUNCHING LOVE AS YOUR CAREER

TAKING STEPS TO START A SUCCESSFUL CAREER THROUGH THE HEART OF PURPOSE

BY

ANGEL LITTLE

TABLE OF CONTENTS

"MY PRAYER TO GOD"

Dear God,

I'm not writing this book for selfish motive, gain or personal bragging rights. I'm writing this book because you laid it on my heart. I humbly come before you, giving you my heartfelt thanks for your unconditional love. I give you my worship and my praise. I pray that those who read this book will be empowered, inspired and blessed. Please send blessings to those that supported me and held me accountable throughout the entire process of writing this book. Thank you for the gift of life and that I may not live in vain. I know that your words and promises stands true and will come to past. Therefore, I ask that everyone in the world will have the opportunity to choose Love.

In Jesus name. Amen.

MY DRIVEN PURPOSE

The purpose for writing this book is so that people all over the world will be inspired to launch Love as their career. By doing so allowing themselves transparency and a better understanding of what it is we should be seeking for and longing for on the journey of being fulfilled into a successful life. Let us with an open heart find out the true meaning of success and not viewing success as the world sees it. Oftentimes we choose a career for what it can do for us instead of what we can do for our career. That's why we are called selfish creatures. Even if we are not aware of it or look at it from a spiritual perspective, we are Heavenly creatures predestined before we were even born so that in this lifetime while we are on this earth, our Heavenly Father will give us the opportunity to make a difference. Not just for others but also for ourselves. When we start looking at life in a way to improve on making a difference in our lives and in the lives of others, then we can ask ourselves. What can I do for my career? I view it this way. If we chase Love through our actions just as much as we chase our careers. Our careers will chase us into a life that we love. Our purpose will be revealed through the mind, our spirit will be stirred through our heart and then will the process of launching Love as your career be initiated into action.

DEDICATION

I would like to dedicate this book to God, who believes in me and trusted me enough to share with others what I learned over the years about choosing to Love as my career. He has blessed me over the years and still is, despite my faults and shortcomings. I thank him for giving me the authentic ideas and words for writing this book. I honor this book in the names of my father, Richard Harper, and my mother Carrie Harper, who were both the best parents in the world. They demonstrated to me, as a young girl, how to have a serving heart for Love. I would like to give my deepest admiration to my sister Laverne and my son Richard who went through health challenges in 2020 during the pandemic. They never left their faith and instead they both had drawn closer to God. I'm thankful and blessed to have my family and friends who supported and encouraged my decision to write this book. I'm blessed to have a church home at True Light Baptist. I thank my internal ailment coach, Joanna Rincon, who motivated and coached me along the process. I would like to also thank my sister in Christ author and Minister, Michelle Murray, who mentored me through the process of writing and publishing my first book. I'm thankful for everyone all over the world, who believe in the power of Unconditional Love.

CHAPTER 1- CHOOSE LOVE

LOVING GOD AND HAVING A RELATIONSHIP WITH HIM

Becoming a new believer is like starting a new chapter in a book. We read it, ponder on it and process the guidelines of being a true believer. A book does not serve its purpose for us to stay on the same page. Therefore, we must follow through every page in order to make it to the next chapter. These actions require being under the Lord's authority through humbleness, submission, and obedience. We are to look at life from God's perspective and not our own. Pursuing his will for our life. There are improvements to be made through humbleness. Relationships to be accommodated through submission. Guidelines to be followed through obedience. Being humble is not being proud or arrogant. It's being wise enough to receive room for improvements in every area of our life. Being submissive is not dominating the relationship, it's giving of yourself enough to accommodate someone else's preference through selflessness. Being obedient is not a state of controlling someone against their will. It's complying with guideline that will sustain structure in your life. Following our creator's will may not seem normal to the world. We may be despised, rejected, and misunderstood, but we can look forward to receiving a heavenly reward! The world may be accustomed to feeling like we must do something to gain a reward. The world may feel obligated to give back in return for receiving a bonus. Although from the very beginning it could have started in our childhood, when we had to so call be on "best behavior" in order to get a gift or a treat from our parents. When reality, I believe if it was explained why these actions are important instead of bribing our behavior, we would better understand the process of how life should work. It's not our parents' fault because they were taught it also. This world treats everything in life as a "supply and demand."

Fortunately, in the spiritual rim, salvation is a free offering. The only thing we must do is be willing to receive salvation. Our Father sent his sinless son Jesus on earth to take the penalty of our sins of wrongdoing because he loves us, and his will is for us to be more like him. After we have accepted salvation through Jesus Christ, it is not the will of our Heavenly Father for us to stay in the position of being a beginning Believer. Becoming a believer is a position that requires continued growth and requires for us to launch into an elevated position. When we accept the responsibility of what salvations offer, we are then on the right path of receiving sanctification. Sanctification will label us as being sacred and holy that will set us apart from the world that is wicked. We can then define a true definition of having a successful life. When we start that new chapter in our life by following Godly principles, we will add the ingredients of a whole new level of love.

LIFESTYLE TO LOVE GOD

1. We must follow God's leadership and work as his disciples

2. We must worship and praise God as we love and trust in him.

3. We must be willing to share our Heavenly Father with others

4. We must allow our mind, body, and spirit to be transformed

5. We must keep hope, joy, and peace, knowing that we will see Jesus Christ someday.

CHAPTER 2 – IN LOVE WITH ME

2.1 - LOVING OURSELVES

When we focus on fear, insecurities, doubts, guilt, and negative thoughts, we tend to get distracted with the direction our life is headed. Fearing God is a positive emotion. We show our respect and admiration to our Heavenly Father because he deserves to be honored. Why? He is the creator of the universe and the fullness thereof. Psalm24:1. However, fear itself is a negative emotion that causes someone to panic and be agitated. Being doubtful causes us to be fearful and uncertain. Guilt is an experience when we do something wrong or compromise our standards. Insecurities are recognized when we feel unconfident, unassured, and inadequate. These emotions bring on our personal negative thoughts of ourselves. We can be our own worst enemy by questioning ourselves. Am I good enough? Of course, you are! Words of advice when thoughts about yourself and spoken words about yourself come to mind. "Don't sabotage your opportunity to accept yourself, care for yourself and to love yourself." There are lifelong learning tools that are required to make a conscious effort to consistently work towards. The knowledge and wisdom of knowing who we are and why we were created will empower us to feel adequate, qualified, and satisfied in the ability to reach our highest potential and set us on the platform that our Heavenly Father has planned for us. 1. **Self-Acceptance** gives you the motivation to feel adequate, qualified, and good enough towards what's in your heart to do. 2. **Self Care** inspires you to feel confident and approved to do what's in your heart to do. 3. **Self Love** intensifies our reasoning for being satisfied, content, pleased and glorifying. These 3 Self guidelines are initiated when we**: 1.** Read what our creator says about us. **2.** Speak positive words in existence even when we don't see it yet. **3.** Help others that are worse off than you are. **Note:** Don't wait until we are personally trying to get it together. We will never be perfect. **4.** Challenge yourself to do something outside your comfort zone and finish it no matter what the outcome is. **5.** Search for at least one thing you like about yourself and appreciate it. **Note:** Use it to your advantage in life. I asked different people many times during life. "What do you like about yourself?" Sadly, and surprisingly, I had those to say, "they like nothing about themselves." I couldn't imagine not having at least one thing to say positive about myself. Hey, we are living in the real world. There are a lot of hurting individuals out here. You may come face to face with them every day and don't even really recognize the person that only feels anything but a broken soul and a broken spirit. When we constantly come across unexpected obstacles, negative situations and circumstances, it can hinder our progress in life. We tend to run away from our challenges and towards what we feel is safe. Turning away from our tasks and what is required of us to reach our destiny will not secure us from going through difficult moments, but instead, it will keep us mentally confined. Which then causes us to remain in mental bondage.

In order to overcome these mental restraints, we can start by thinking of solutions instead of focusing on the problem. Anything negative that is beyond our control may be a challenge but coming up with other options that we can control will bring advancement to the way we think and how we handle a situation. If you want to launch love as your career, embrace self-love with self-approval.

2.2-DEVELOPING QUALITIES IN OURSELVES

In order to love ourselves, we must develop certain qualities that would add meaning to our self-worth and keep us free for the rest of our lives by:

>Enforcing a healthy mindset of ourselves.

>Speaking positive words in our dialogue.

>Leading by example if we want to make a difference.

CHAPTER 3 – BEING A GIVER

3.1 – LOVING OTHERS EVEN WHEN OTHERS DON'T LOVE US BACK.

Loving others even when they don't love us back is one of the biggest challenges and concerns, we face in life. When dealing with these issues, we either convince ourselves that we don't care at all, or we become angry and bitter and wish to retaliate. These negative feelings cause resentment, which leads to seeking revenge. Loving others regardless of the way they feel about us and treat us releases these harmful emotions that can become trapped in our minds. However, the grace and mercy that our Heavenly Father gives us should motivate us to love even when it feels unfair. We cannot self-promote love in our human strength. Therefore, we must rely on God's supernatural strength to get us there. Instead of rehearsing wrongful experiences in our minds, we should ask the Heavenly Father to help us and enable us to launch the process of transforming love into our hearts.

3.2 – HERE ARE SOME ACTION STEPS WE CAN TAKE TO BECOME A GENUINE GIVER

Mentor others

You don't necessarily have to be a parent, a teacher, or a counselor to be a mentor. You may even feel like you don't deserve or have the qualities of being a mentor. But, that is quite untrue. Throughout our life, even as a young child. We all have experienced something that can be helpful and shared with someone even in our life's worst experiences. By educating someone who is willing to learn what you are willing to teach, will give that person a better outlook on their situation by them knowing that they are not the first and they are not alone. Let's not look at mentoring as a designated person's job but rather a position that requires shared responsibility.

Pray for others

Often when we pray, we tend to pray to our Heavenly Father solely about ourselves, not thinking about the huge world out there and the countless people that are so in desperate need of our prayers. The bitter truth is that we like to criticize others instead of praying for them and their guidance. We should not approach our Heavenly Father with a negative attitude and a prideful heart when we pray for others. It may seem at times that someone is undeserving of your prayers, but being humble before God and asking Him to help and guide others will be a selfless thing to do. It also helps us with the healing process of forgiveness and induces the heart to love. Also

When we pray for others. We should rely on the Holy Spirit, as we ask God to help us to recognize our own flaws and selfishness through our imperfection as he encourages us to make transformational changes to better ourselves for progressive growth. Have you ever seen a person on the side of a highway having some sort of problem with their car? Have you ever seen the opportunity to pray for the person or persons on the side of the highway that had an accident? In that moment, did you at least take out a few seconds to ask God to protect them and help them with their situation? If you never have and never even thought of it. You can start launching love as your career by developing these essential habits into your daily routine so that a positive habit plus an effective prayer will equal a quality life.

Visit others

I know you have a demanding job that requires your full attention and that you have other stuff going on, but I'm sure we can try at least once a month to connect with someone. Even a phone call that can express our concern for someone else is adequate to make the other person realize their significance in your life. Don't think about whether the person would do the same for you in return, but just do it out of the kindness of your heart.

Volunteer at homeless shelters, animal shelters, habitat for humanity, and nursing homes

Volunteering for older people and having an interest in pets perhaps might not really be your thing, but they have food banks, shelters, and other options that might interest you. Spending your time and efforts doing these things will help you feel like you have a purpose in life and that your presence matters while creating a lot of positive impacts around your surroundings. We may not necessarily have a particular talent, gift, brilliance, or skill to offer our service in every area. However, if we are willing, our Heavenly Father will enhance our ability to do what is necessary even if we feel that we are not capable of doing it.

Help those who are less fortunate

The reality of it is, that there is someone out there who is less fortunate than we are. Not just that, but there are people in hospitals battling for their lives. There are people at home, yet they can't do anything for themselves, but if you are like me, that considers yourself to be very fortunate and is able to do whatever we mostly desire. We can surely assist those that are unfortunate. There are some people that have no one who cares for them. There are people who get no visits, no phone calls and no expression of love. Considering the situation of these people, we are blessed by the grace of God to have a home, feel safe, more than enough food, in good health, and surrounded by love. I can guarantee that when we take the focus off ourselves and are willing to help someone less fortunate than us, we will begin to feel humbled and blessed where we are. We would be able to truly acknowledge how blessed we are once we see the realization of another person's life rather than perceiving what we hear from others or making our own judgment about a person and their situation. Would we like to see better for ourselves? Absolutely. When we recognize and appreciate our blessings, it will give us a sense of hope and faith in our creator and create a heart of thanksgiving and gratefulness to our Heavenly Father.

Financial giving

If we are not able to give our time which, in my opinion, is very beneficial in serving others. Another opportunity can be considered. Which is helping others financially. There are many organizations out there in the world whose fundamental aim is to help communities. Without our help and the concern for those that are struggling, we will not be launching love as our career. One of my favorite organizations is St. Jude Children Hospital, the Atlanta Food Bank and Meals on Wheels, because I love the objective behind their missions. Heartening yourself to help others financially, you can always search around to find out which organization inspires you to help the most.

At an early age, I was taught to give. My foundation was laid on a collection plate during Sunday School. My parents always believed in making certain that my sister and I had some form of currency before leaving home to attend church service. We didn't give much as younger kids, but we were learning consistency in our giving and investing in the community in which we believed in and lived. We are all blessed with certain talents and gifts in which to give. Some of us may even have more than one. We can use these talents and gifts more purposefully by launching a heart of service. Whenever you feel like there is a need, or wherever you see there is a need, and however there is a way to give in need, there will be opportunities for us to present our service by giving. When we are led by Jesus's examples, we all have a personal responsibility on this earth. When our Heavenly Father assigns us to do something within His will, and we move forward in obedience with a righteous motive, Our Heavenly Father will show us what to do and give us the ability and equip us to do it. Even during times of doubt and fear of carrying out His will, our willingness and commitment to obey will strengthen our faith and give us the confidence to achieve His purpose in our life. An act of genuine service leads to advancement in our life by impacting and inspiring others to give back through our compassion, concern, empathy, and love towards others. Whether it's in the workplace, church, volunteering, or leisure time, our service opens the opportunity to tell others about the Heavenly Father.

It gives us the gift of personal satisfaction and peace within. It also gives us the gift of joy, knowing that our Heavenly Father is being glorified and He is pleased with our performance in life.

I don't boast about what I do for others because I serve in the name of our Heavenly Father, and it's a blessing showing love for others. I would like to give an example of how we can show love for others, not expecting anything in return, because it's just a blessing to be able to bless someone else. In the year 2020, the Covid-19 impacted the nation. This pandemic adversely affected me as well. Not only did my beautiful mother, whom I will cherish for the rest of my days, passed away, but something distressful happened too. A month later, my employer called me and told me that even though I was a valuable employee, my position had been eliminated after 23 years of serving in hospitality. As shocking as this may sound. I was disappointed, yet not devastated as most would have assumed, including myself. I felt at peace, which we will talk more in detail about the spirit. Giving you a short version of myself to say during the pandemic.

Even though I was at home, staying busy around the house, I found a way to be of service to others. I made use of a few volunteering opportunities with my son, Richard. I also had a neighbor who's in her 90's. She didn't ask me at first, but I saw a need. Whenever I would go visit her, she would mention her hair. I'm saying to myself, "I'm not a hairstylist, but I know how to comb hair." As time passed by, I became her personal hairstylist. It was certain that she could not cook anymore. Therefore, I would sometimes offer to cook her something during the week.

Another example of how I served during a challenging time of my life was when an elderly friend whom I met through visiting a church member who could no longer stay by herself and eventually had to stay in a nursing home. After she passed away, I continued to visit the home. It got to the point that the elderly person who became my friend wanted something different to eat every now and then outside of the nursing home. I started cooking fish sandwiches to bring whenever I came to visit. It's amazing how even the simplest of things can make a person appreciate life. Think very seriously of what it would possibly be like not being able to do things freely anymore because of an unfortunate circumstance. We must be compassionate enough and empathize with those that are not able to do for themselves. I'm not saying that this will be your specialty to manage but we all have some sort of physical ability to give. Whether it's using our mouth to encourage others. And even a smile, a hug, and encouraging words are a way of contributing our gifts and talents to serve. Have you ever thought to yourself how it would feel to not be able to do much for yourself or let alone have no one to come visit you and seem to not care about you? Just like the pastor and spiritual singer Dietrich Haddon would sing the words, "If you don't have love, you ain't got nothing."

CHAPTER 4 – LOVE IN ITS ESSENCE

4.1 - WHAT IS LOVE?

Love is an intense feeling, a great interest, a deep attachment or affection to something or someone. Love commits. Love desires to express itself through kindness, patience, respect, forgiveness, faithfulness and loving unconditionally. Love hurts when someone else hurts, Love thinks of the other person's feelings, and Love is not all about "I" because it is selfless.

Love does not cause one to envy; it does not boast, it's not prideful, it does not easily anger, it does not count your mistakes, it does not delight in evil, it does not pay back, but instead, it gives back.

4.2 - WHAT HAPPENS WHEN THERE IS NO LOVE?

We become detached from ourselves and others, which leads to bitterness, division, resentment, hate, anger, violence, pride, jealousy, selfishness, and indifference.

4-3 – WHAT HAPPENS WHEN THERE IS LOVE?

We become connected with ourselves and others, which leads to sweetness, unity, contentment, love, friendliness, kindness, humbleness, admiration, selflessness and agreeable.

4.4 - WHAT IS A CAREER

It is a profession within a specific area in a person's life that allows opportunities for progression and growth while excelling through discipline, systems, education, instructions, coaching, teaching, mentoring, tasks, assignments, strength, ability, achievements, faithfulness, determination, dependability, accountability, perseverance, resilience, and skills.

4.5– LAUNCH

Launching means to start, begin, and break into your true form.

4.6 - MIND

The way we perceive things and what we think about is essential. Nothing about us will change until we are ready and willing to change our negative thoughts and the way we view things. Our thoughts and the way we think can remind us of painful memories, failures from our past and sabotage our positive thoughts by keeping us in fear of an uncertain future. Our thoughts may also determine our actions. Have you ever made it a habit to think and speak on positive things repeatedly to the point that you could see them? Have you ever had negative thoughts and have spoken negative words repeatedly to the point that you believed it? Our state of mind works in the same manner. It's like going to work every day. We are in such a habit mode; we already know what is expected of us. We get up at a certain time; we take a shower, we get dressed up, we groom ourselves, and off to work, we go with our daily routines. We know exactly where to start when we get to work. Some of us even have to have a cup of coffee before starting work. We even exhibit a certain attitude before entering the workplace.

There are rules in the workplace, an order of conduct, and discipline to be maintained. It's good to be intentional with our thoughts and monitor the way we think. We have to program our minds to think positively, train ourselves to be disciplined, and practice self-control. Our mind will go where we allow it to go. Our thoughts will form as much as you allow them to grow. When we are on social media, Facebook, Instagram, and Twitter every day, we allow ourselves to be consumed by what we see and how we should be. Only to realize that what we see most of the time is not always true but a false PowerPoint. I would suggest creating a mental spreadsheet in your mind by launching your day with a prayer to our Heavenly Father. If you have not reached that part of your spiritual life yet, please make it one of your tasks to meditate on positive thoughts about yourself to achieve a new way to process your way of thinking. Unlike relying on negative emotions how we feel but renewing our mind to think the way we are created to be. Romans 12:2 in the bible resource guide talks about restoring our state of mind so that we won't burden ourselves with the way the world views life. Our thinking can be transformed and acceptable to our Heavenly Father the way he views life's success, for this is His will for us to be successful and not be defeated. We are not to observe the way the world looks at success but how our creator views our success. Realistically, I'm not saying that we must wake up and feel full of happiness every single day, but we can have the supernatural strength and the capability to coach ourselves out of our negative thoughts and have authority over the way we feel by allowing our positive thinking skills to lead us into thinking positively and speaking positively. If you work a morning shift, you may have to get up a little early to attend our Heavenly Father's meeting by launching prayer and meditation. When you receive a positive, healthy, refreshing start in the morning, you tend to think better. Not to mention whenever negative spirits come our way that day, we are able to conquer our enemy. In Isaiah 54:17, God's words say, "No weapon formed against me shall prosper." I advise a commitment towards our efforts to stay faithful, motivated, inspired, determined, and focused. We should constantly remind ourselves that our mind is our computer and whatever data we program information inside our computer, whether negative or positive. It's the results that are going to print out of our mouth and into our actions. Choosing to have a fruitful life will bring forth a driven outcome of self-discipline and perseverance. We can't move forward into a positive lifestyle while thinking at the same time of negative thoughts. It's a fact that the more you practice something and continue doing it, the further advance your way of thinking will become and your actions will follow. The mind is a battlefield, a place where there is conflict. Our mind is also very powerful. That's why we have the authority to decide to allow our thoughts to be in control by God's truth, or we can allow the enemy, which is Satan, to deceive us from the truth about ourselves.

Satan (evil spirits) deceives the world by having us to believe that having pride, power, fame, and being opulent are the highest of reaching goals, but once you get in a relationship with our Heavenly Father and learn his truths, God begins to show us the true meaning of success. If you want to have a fulfilling life that chooses your career, you must create a solid foundation by using the right materials for building relationships. We first launch Love as our career by trusting and depending on the right source, our Heavenly Father. We must start the process by taking time out of our busy schedules to get to know him. When we get to know him, we learn not to depend on ourselves, but we are taught to depend on our Heavenly Father. We then can gain the education that we need through his word by faithfully showing our Love towards him. My question is, would you choose to have a one-way relationship with someone? I hope you said no. In this case, how do you think our Heavenly Father feels when he tries to have a relationship with us? We give him no time, no thought, no attention, no thanksgiving except on the day of the holiday, no praise, no worship and basically no love. Whether we do it on purpose or are just not aware, we are rejecting his Love for us. The difference about our Heavenly Father is him, loving us so much. He tries to get our attention through others. He wants us to share some of our time with him. He wants to have conversations with us, provide for us, heal us, and fight our battles. Our Heavenly Father is a jealous God (Exodus 34:14), and he always allows his grace and mercy to be upon us. Meaning that he loves us and gives us his favor of life even though we may not deserve it. Loving our creator as we get to know the real meaning of Love, we become entitled to love ourselves despite our own flaws. How we love ourselves grants us the ability to be able to love others, love when it's not expressed back in return, Love when it is not deserving, and love others that seem indifferent just because we feel they don't fit our standards.

4.7 - ATTITUDE

When we allow our mind to think and wonder in a certain way, whether it is negative or positive more than likely, it will surface. Your attitude determines if you will choose a career that is best suited for your lifestyle. It has been quoted in the Bible in Proverbs Chapter 23:7. "As a man thinks in his heart, so is he." A positive attitude brings on good results as opposed to a negative attitude that will set you up for failure only to find out that you can't move forward in your life's career. Matthew 7:19 "A good tree produces good fruit, and a bad tree produces bad fruit." Our lives move in the directions into which we think. That is why it is wise to shape your thinking on what you know is the truth and not what you feel is the truth. In order to know the truth, we have to pick up our resource book (the Holy book) and study it daily if not, consistently. Ask yourself, where are your thoughts leading you? Are you having a mind of worrying thoughts, or are you having a mind of peaceful thoughts? Are you having a mind of negative thoughts, or are you having a mind of positive thoughts? Are you having worldly thoughts, or are you having a mind of eternal thoughts?

Worrying thoughts

Keeps you feeling fearful, anxious, stressed, hopeless, and doubtful, discouraged, depressed, and distressed, which leads to sickness in your body.

Peaceful thoughts

Keeps you feeling restful, pleasant, calm, secure, and safe, which leads to a joyful, fulfilling, and healthy lifestyle.

Negative thoughts

Keeps you feeling insecure, deceived, uncertain, mistrustful, distrustful, useless, undeserving, worthless, hopeless, inadequate, frustrated, guilty, which leads to a lifestyle of jealousy, anger, strife, lovelessness, desperation, and intimidation.

Positive thoughts

Keeps you feeling hopeful, joyful, loved, energetic, motivated, determined, generous, inspired, adequate, resilient, and competent, which leads to a successful lifestyle.

Worldly thoughts

Keeps you feeling defeated, weak, indifferent, prejudiced, oppressed, offended, cheated, abused, and insulted, which leads to a lifestyle of betrayal, shamefulness, hurt, pitifulness, abandonment, and violation?

Eternal thoughts

Keeps us feeling comforted, peaceful, loving, secure, faithful, empowered, strong, hopeful, humble, appreciative, grateful, compassionate, thankful, kindhearted, which leads to a satisfying lifestyle.

Personal Growth

If we want to further our success in life, we must be willing to grow. Being successful as launching Love as your career goes far beyond making lots of money, pursuing to be popular, seemingly to be better than others. As I was growing up, I always thought that being successful was about having a nice car, having a nice size house, wearing nice clothes, looking a certain way, and having a good-paying job. I'm not knocking these things, but these things do not make you and me who we really are and who God created us to be. It's not what others think of us, but it's how our Heavenly

Father thinks of us, which should inspire us on how we think of ourselves. God created you and me for his purpose and his will. He has given us instructions on how to live. We all have assignments. Every individual has their own different unique assignments, and even though they are different, we all are to aim towards one goal. Through God's words and living through obedience and purpose, he wants to mentor us to love and serve others. Without these essential contributions to life on earth, we are not experiencing success as we should, and we are not launching Love as our career. We are just serving life for a job that is meaningless and will not last. Have you ever thought to ask yourself, "How do you identify yourself?" As I matured mentally, I've wised up to know that I cannot identify myself through someone else. I was created only for my purpose, my will, and my destiny. Please stop comparing yourself to others. It's a positive thing when you admire a person, and you respect where they are in life. However, you don't know how they got to where they are and what they have gone through to get there. We are just looking from the outer glass, wishing we could get in. Have you ever prayed to the Almighty Heavenly Father and sat down with your creator, who gave us life that we may have it more abundantly? (Matthew 10:10) The one who chose us to work for his kingdom will give us the ability to be the best we can be as we continue to discover who we are in him. (Jeremiah 1:5) assures us that we were created for a purpose. Search on your own mental computer wherever you are in life right now. Ask yourself. How do you classify yourself as a person? What changes, if any, would you have to make to see improvements about yourself? Will you be content with your decision? Make notes on the line below and meditate on your answers.

Check-your-self notes:

_____

_____

_____

_____

Key Notes: Without essential contributions to life on earth, we are not Launching Love as Our

Career. We are just serving life as a job that is meaningless and will not last.

CHAPTER 5 - POWERLESS

If you see no room for improvements in your database, then I suggest connecting with our Creator and ask Him to guide you where development is needed in your life. By doing so, you will discover that there is much more to yourself that needs advancing.

5.1 - CHOOSING TO REACH YOUR POTENTIAL WHEN YOUR SITUATION SEEMS TO LEAVE YOU POWERLESS

Everyone makes mistakes along the way in their life, but the real question is whether you will make decisions and take actions that will leave you with regret? Will the fear of making a mistake leave you enslaved to not growing and reaching your greatest potential?

I know what has helped me along the way as I continue to grow. Is not focused on who people think I should be. I'm serving a purpose on earth that is not meant for someone else but only for what is designed for me. I believe once we get that in the process of our thinking, there will be less stress and pressure about life when striving to reach our full potential. We can't always control what happens in our life, but we can control how we handle it. Let's consider something very simple as an example. If we pray before leaving home to have a safe trip, then within moments of getting on the highway, we realize we are stuck in traffic. Why would we get all bent out of shape? Why do we start banging on the steering wheel, possible road-raging, or even give someone a bad facial gesture when we pray for a safe journey? We must appreciate how God, through his grace, has honored our prayer by keeping us at a standstill until the coast is clear. Not to mention, we probably should have prepared to leave a little sooner to give ourselves extra time anyway. If we are asking God for something and it's out of our control, we must be willing to trust him in the situation even when we don't understand it.

Proverbs 3:5 says "Trust in the Lord with all your heart and lean not on your own understanding. In all your ways submit to him and he will direct your path." We must thank God for his goodness in all situations and thank him for what could have negatively happened but didn't happen.

I personally love this scripture and I love this prayer because when you meditate on it and focus on the words, it really gives you comfort. "God grant me the serenity to accept the things I cannot change; courage to change the things I can, and Wisdom to know the difference."

If there is a job that you are currently at and you don't feel like it's the job for you, try having a positive attitude by thanking our Heavenly Father for the income instead. In the meantime, ask God to lead you into a new direction in your life's journey. A journey that has a purpose and chasing your heart with passion. I heard someone say that God is no Genie, but I know for myself that he is a way maker, miracle worker, and a promise keeper. When we are trusting in our Heavenly Father for promotion, we should be patient and wait with expectancy and belief that we will be moved to our divine assignment. Our waiting moments can be more productive by fasting in the process.

By fasting and through prayer, our thinking will become wiser, our hearing will become sharper, and our vision will become clearer. Even our desire for God will be awakened, and the discernment of his direction will be revealed. We will have the insight to set aside earthly concerns and concentrate on heavenly matters so that we can get a better understanding of our Heavenly Father's plans and purpose for our life. Also, during the process of fasting, we may be able to identify some root causes of our non-spiritual growth that can contribute to our heart failing to love. When we fast, we will be able to block out unnecessary distractions and have the capability to stay focused on hearing our Heavenly Father's voice through our spiritual abilities. Prayer gets the job done and its purpose is set out to accomplish positive change in many different areas in our life. For our prayers to be powerful and effective, we must align our requests with our Heavenly Father's will and be in an agreement with him. By doing so, we must learn God's character such as: who he is, the way he thinks, and how he works. Through these principles, our Heavenly Father may have to delete some of the junk in our inbox because our spiritual email will conflict with our sinful attitudes and behavior and cause conviction to take place. The reasons for fasting will give us the dependence to focus and trust in our Father's plan with a righteous motive while praying will give us confidence through his faithfulness. There are many books and information on ways of fasting. One of my most favorite books on fasting, which I highly recommend, is written by Jentzen Franklin.

We all need some sort of income to pay our bills and to live. No matter where you are working, whether you are an entrepreneur serving yourself or serving in someone else's company, we are still in the business of serving others. You must stay focused mentally on your pathway to success. In all things, it takes kindness, patience, service, forgiveness and love. Do you need to read that again? In all things, it takes kindness, patience, service, forgiveness, and love.

I know you must be thinking to yourself about how we can show love when people are mistreating us by being disrespectful, mean, unfair, argumentative, and difficult; basically, the opposite of showing love. I would be sitting here not being truthful if I told you that it is easy and that sometimes we would never fail at showing love. However, 1. Knowing who we are working for which is the Almighty Heavenly Father is the key. He asked us to show kindness, peace, patience, forgiveness and Love. Galatians 5:22, 23. He would not ask us to do anything that he thought we would not be capable to do. We must believe that if we would put Godly scriptures into practice and trust in his promises, he will work things out for our good. Romans 8:28 "All things work together for the good to those that love God and are called according to his purpose." I can write this book on my behalf because I know what he has done and what he will continue to do for me, he will do it for any other person. We must be intentional at launching love as our career if we want to see results. I read this hanging on my sister's wall which made a whole lot of sense to me.

"Your mind is a garden,

Your thoughts are the seeds,

You can grow flowers, or you can grow weeds"

Remember when we talked about the conflicts going on in our mind? If we are not able to identify what is going on in our mind, heart, and soul, it will be challenging to defeat our opposition. When we are not working on daily responsibilities that are required of us, we develop negative thinking. Negative thinking creates a war in our mind. Once that war continues, it causes a stronghold, which leads to a wrong pattern of thinking and keeps us from being mentally free. This domino affects us emotionally which turns into bitter, hate, strife, and anger. Eventually, these strongholds surface and become revealed which are then expressed through our actions. This is the reason for reading God's scriptures daily, meditate and think on positive quotes to keep you grounded during difficult times. As we aim towards accomplishing our goals to successful living, we will go through hardship, and it may take us through setbacks to get us on course. When it does, we can be prepared to fight back and not be defeated. We can be resilient and continue the route to our destiny.

Fruitless Thoughts: It takes too much effort and pressure when we doubt our abilities and when our minds are focused on our limitations instead of our Heavenly Father. We have in our mind that we are inadequate to complete the tasks. Sometimes we can be our own worst enemy and critic by feelings of envy, intimidation, unworthiness, underserving and self-condemnation. Ephesians 2:10 tells us that we are God's masterpiece. We were created in Jesus Christ to do good work. Another favorite scripture of mine, which I suggest we meditate on when we are feeling a sense of inadequacy or lack of being qualified to do something, is read Philippians 4:13. "I can do all things through Christ who strengthens me." We would want to make the necessary changes in our minds. What happens when we get a new mindset? We find out that we are important and that we matter, but guess what? All Lives Matter! Our mind stores powerful knowledge if we feed it and God's words are our most powerful weapon. We must use it if we want to fight against the war in our mind. We must fight against the thoughts that keep us in bondage and try to defeat us mentally. We can cancel the contract of negative thinking and pursue positive thinking by launching love as your career.

Fruitful Thought: When I believe and trust in God: He is always working things out for my good. Romans 8:28. I don't regret where I been and how far he has brought me to get where I am. I just feel blessed beyond measure to have the opportunity to spend time with family, take care of my parents in my later years and be the best daughter and parent I knew how to be while enjoying the journey of being able to serve in the hospitality industry.

5.2 - MAKING IMPROVEMENTS FOR GROWTH RATHER THAN OUTSIDE CHANGE FOR IMAGE

Changes for our image more than improvements for our growth can be dangerous. Why? The inner self matters the most. What's on the inside reflects the outside no matter how good the outside looks. Have you ever seen sexy people's appearance on the outside, but when you meet their fatalistic behavior, their looks start to change? However, improvements with your personal growth are about having the mindset to reach your highest potential in all areas of your life. I think this is very essential because when we stay in that same mindset, we tend to hold ourselves back from becoming someone greater. It's amazing and so true when I heard the statement, "people are so anxious to improve their circumstances, but are unwilling to improve themselves." It is our responsibility to make the necessary improvements within ourselves. The longer we wait or hesitate to change things on the inside, the greater our chances get that we won't ever make the change. Don't wait on a feeling of motivation or to get inspired, just get in the mindset of making it happen. When we are depending on doing something only when we are in the mood or when it is convenient, we lose the development part of growing a consistent habit. Improving ourselves daily opens the doors of possibilities, options, opportunities, and the potential of continued growth. We can start off with something small and realistic. Something that will challenge us on a consistent basis. I'm not talking about getting your nails done weekly or getting a haircut once a week. I'm talking about something more profound. I'm referring to limiting yourself to a food item that you know is not good for you just by starting off at least once a week. Even showing a smile to someone once a week even if smiling is not your thang! When we apply ourselves and make the effort to work on our patience, stay persistent, disciplined and consistent once a week. Our habits will ultimately cause personal growth and over a period, with these attributes in mind. All things will start off challenging and won't be easy, but they will become manageable. In other words, instead of focusing on changing yourself as your goal, let's focus more on the reasons and the benefits that our lives will profit from just by making lifestyle adjustments. When we demonstrate positive changes in our daily lives, hopefully we will gain the right attitude of doing things for the right reasons with the right motives behind it. Making a commitment to our development is like reading a thick book with many pages. Once we keep reading it consistently, the pages become less and eventually we will finish it. Then there's another book to discover. I also would like to encourage everyone to nourish their faith by reading God's words and meditating on his promises. This will allow us to hold ourselves accountable for a change of growth on the inside rather than outside change for our image.

Evaluation process: It is our duty, job, and responsibility to take inventory of ourselves. That's where growth steps in. Inventory is a checklist of things that are noted during the evaluation process that needs to be stocked, restocked or replenished. If necessary, we need to remove whatever that is not needed or that is outdated.

5.3 - THINGS THAT NEED TO BE STOCKED, RESTOCKED AND REPLENISHED

Optimistic Mindset

Positive Attitude

Power of a Righteous Tongue

Beneficial Impact

Choosing Love

5.4 - THINGS THAT ARE NOT NEEDED OR OUTDATED

Pessimistic Mindset

Negative Attitude

Bad Mouthing

Callous Impact

Choosing to Hate

5.5 - LAUNCHING LOVE WITH THESE FOUR ESSENTIAL STEPS AS YOUR CAREER

Motivation

Deals with the mind

Is it a determined attempt to do something? It starts with a willing mind. In order to get anything accomplished or achieved, we must be empowered through prayer, discipline, determination, perseverance, faithfulness, motivation, and reliance on our Heavenly Father to enable us through his words, and with his supernatural strength.

Effort

Deals with the body

We should make a daily commitment to remain under our Heavenly Father's authority by surrendering ourselves to obey his will to please him, and not man.

Passion

Deals with the spirit

A powerful emotion that one feels about something or someone. This emotion causes us to place strong interest in. Our Heavenly Father loves us so passionately that he sent his son Jesus Christ on earth to save those who are willing to be accepted in the family of the True Light and to teach Christ like attributes, so that we will have a chance to live with the Heavenly Father eternally.

Communication

Deals with relationships

It starts with talking, listening and spending time with our Heavenly Father, friends, family, loved ones, and those who we may encounter. Treating others as we want to be treated helps build an intimate and satisfying relationship that people desire to have. Without healthy relationships, life lacks meaning regardless of all the things that we possess.

CHAPTER 6 – INVESTING IN OURSELVES BY BELIEVING I CAN

When I started reading one of my collections of books, it came to mind as being true. When we discover what we are put on this earth for, it becomes a whole new way of seeing life. Once I discovered it, my thinking became super profound. It was like an awakening of the heart. It was as if my gift was stirred, and I had fallen in love all over again. One of the quotes that I read was, "The two most significant days in a person's life are, the day we were born into the world and the day we discover the purpose of why we are here." If we think of one of the saddest things to discover, it would be to imagine someone out there living their entire life without ever knowing why they are really on this earth. It's just a constant roller coaster for some, and when their life is over, well…that just means the ride is over and it's time to get off to let someone else take your spot. The difference is when we know the reasons for being put on this earth, we can leave this earth knowing that we can pass the torch to our next generation, knowing there was purpose being fulfilled for us being here.

6.1 - LESSON TO BE LEARNED

The message I learned, which I now wish to convey, is how I was motivated by my thoughts. I want to hold myself accountable for growth through my actions. I needed to take more initiative than what I was doing and push myself to be intentional about coming up with a plan of action daily in order to strive at getting things done and knowing at the end of the day it will bring me joy and satisfaction.

When you start off your day in an organized manner by penning down all the things you need to be doing, it gives you a sense of control and inner tranquility. Moreover, once you get done with your list at the end of the day, you feel accomplished, productive, and as if you've completed a task that brings inner fulfillment. However, one mustn't get discouraged, if their to-do list doesn't get finished the day it was created, they should feel proud about the fact that they have at least started it.

6.2 - ACTION PPP'S- STRATEGIZE YOUR ACTIONS

Spreadsheet that will bring your Blueprint to Reality

In order to make a change, we must be willing to change our environment. Be intentional about spending time with positive people and interacting with people that want to learn and grow. Surrounding yourself with people who believe that they can grow will improve your mindset as well! Being around those that aim towards purpose is contagious. The morale surrounding our life goes up, our energy is sparked, and our view becomes clearer. We need to take a step to create a spreadsheet for a different path that we had before, so that we can formulate a different blueprint of our lives. Looking forward to something always gives us energy. So why don't we look forward to making a change by making a difference in the world, starting with ourselves?

What we normally do is we tell ourselves that for some reason that we're not aware of, if we keep doing the same things all over again to get where we want to be, we will eventually get results. While this method is what a lot of people follow in order to move ahead, the disappointing news is that it does not work that way. If we want to see things really change in our personal life we must stop blaming others and make some changes within ourselves.

Changing our life starts with changing our thinking. Sometimes, we may have to face our unknown, overthink our doubts, and conquer our fears. But we must keep in mind that if we change our thinking and neglect to change our actions, we may lose the opportunity to awaken our dreams, and be all that we can potentially be.

6.3-PLAN YOUR PRIORITIES AROUND YOUR PURPOSE

In order to launch a successful plan, you must list your priorities around your purpose. Here are a few essential steps to guide you through the process.

System- pushing yourself by arranging your priorities in an effective way and proactively checking off your agenda daily through discipline in order to produce future goals.

Organize- organizing your life by starting to prepare a set of personal goals and arranging your priorities as it relates to the purpose of your achievements.

Action- taking action by taking risks and focusing your attention on what has to be done and finding it necessary to put forth every effort that will get our personal goals accomplished.

Plan- a detailed blueprint implementing a system that will help incorporate your vision into existence.

Consistent- sticking with a plan by strategizing your platform and being persistent with a system to stay organize and be intentional with your actions and wise with your planning.

Manage- eliminating having a bossy mentality, but being that someone that leads, encourages, motivates and inspires others to reach their potential. Obtaining healthy relationships while caring for those we lead in order to continue learning. Growing in the process while contributing knowledge that will possibly open doors for those that are interested in advancing.

Character- Our nature originates within us. It is our responsibility to change what is necessary and make improvements where is needed in our life.

Application- applying the tools of life to be a opportunity to grow and make a difference. We have a choice in choosing to make a difference. Why not embrace the challenges we will face in life, while undergoing the process of development?

Comfort Zone- be willing to step outside what you feel is comfortable for you or familiar, safe, or secure. Stop making excuses and be resilient by expanding yourself to do something unfamiliar by experimenting and participating in something positive you have never done before.

Innovation- think outside the box. Get creative by creating an idea and mastering a plan to improve your performance through the development of personal growth.

If you follow even a few of the steps above, it will help you to percept life from a totally new point of view. It will give you an optimistic approach to solutions and enhance your mood. Furthermore, it will enable you to launch love as your career.

DISCOVERING WHO I AM WHEN I AM FORCED TO FACE MYSELF

I would like to share another story of how life can change when we persevere through self-action. During the pandemic, there were very limited positions available which affected my job drastically. Everything was mostly shut down especially in the hospitality business. Specifically, restaurants and hotels. There were no more seeing about mom and dad who died to unrelated causes of COVID. There was no more looking after my kids because they had grown up and become independent. Now there was no one left to take charge of but myself. I was stuck with myself. No friends and family to be around because of social distancing. There comes a time in everyone's life, whether it's your younger years or older years. You will eventually become roommates with yourself. You will come face to face with yourself and be forced to live together and have the benefit of viewing your life on how it really is. Whether good or not so good. The reality of finding out who you really are when no one else is around. The reality of taking the responsibility of depending on yourself because there is no one else that will believe in you until you can believe in yourself. I'm talking about that if you don't change to make a better you, situations will remain the same. I was able to discover my insecurities and why I wasn't where I could be in life. I had the wrong mindset, and my actions were unacceptable. I realize that I had to face my insecurities which started way back in my childhood. My sister and I would play games with the kids in the neighborhood. It seemed that I was never that good at the games we played. My bicycling was wack and rolling skating had my back. I always felt that I never came in on top. I was picked on about everything I did. Even though I had a cute face, I was teased on as having the ugliest and skinniest looking legs. I would always laugh it off, but in the inside, it was always stuck in my mind what I was teased about. It was feeling this way leading up throughout my teenage years. I was even bullied in elementary school by my best friend, at least whom I thought was my best friend. If I did accomplish anything. It wasn't because I thought I was good enough to achieve it, but it was because it was by chance and fate that placed me there. Therefore, when I was afraid to do something, I would just shut myself down mentally and talk myself out of it. I didn't realize that the more I put myself down in my thoughts, the more I was terminating my actions to follow through. During the roommate time with myself. I took the initiative to listen to motivatonal speakers, I listened to inspirational music. I exercised. I experimented with cooking and following recipes and meditated on the words and promises of our creator. I was sick and tired of limiting my thoughts on what I could accomplish. I was ready to find out who I really was and who I could become just by knowing the truth, why others are able to make their ideas come to reality and not me. I know that we all are created differently with different desires to succeed, but I also knew that we all have the benefits of stirring our gifts in a way of making a difference. I now have discovered who I am by being forced to face myself that caused me to invest in myself by believing that I can

CHAPTER 7 – LOVE YOUR BODY

We talked about the mind, now let's talk of our body. Our bodies are like a precious wrapped box. We focus on the outside appearance before we even get the chance to figure out what's on the inside of the box. We assume that the bigger the box, must be better. We judge a person on how much they look like they have instead of focusing on the real present inside. We have gotten caught up in to what we see and not what's real, to the point that we would rather have the outside look better than what is on the inside. A gift is something that is given without having to pay for it. That is how our life is. When we were formed in our mother's womb at a designated time, we were born into the world and that's when life became an unwrapped gift. A gift from the creator, the Heavenly Father. We look at our body as our own property, but our body is created to be used for God's purpose. Therefore, there is a way we should be proactive when taking care of our bodies. What does love to have to do with your body? If we love our body and prepare our body for the purpose it was given, we can use it wisely and more effectively in order to live a successful lifestyle. Loving our body should become more of a self-approved by God rather than displaying our body on a resume as entertainment. Whoever, would want a gift that they could not use? That gift would either be tossed aside and never used or given to someone else who may not value it. When we talk about our gifts and talents, our Heavenly Father works in a different way. Our Father will take whatever gift he has given us individually and glorify himself through us. Once he exhibits his gift in us through his eyes, we don't have to be concerned with someone else's gift, because our gifts and talents of purpose will deliberately grant us joy, peace, and satisfaction with our own individual contribution to ourselves and the world. Our creator gives each of us a gift to use for his glory. Even though we have the liberty to conduct our body the way we choose, we will still be held accountable for our actions. If we differentiate the two, a career is something you work towards in one's life with opportunities to progress and growth, that leads to the fulfillment of your purpose. Entertainment is done in one's life for leisure time and pleasure, lasting only for a period of time, which shows no ending results for purpose. Let's make it clear that I have nothing against entertainment that is conducted into the innocence of performance. However, our body should be treated as a cherished temple because it is one of the most essential parts of having the ability to progress and grow. It takes motivation to get us into the habit of progression, which leads to growth. If we feed ourselves with God's substance and use the materials that he has provided for us which is the word of God, not only will our minds be transformed, but our body will be exhibited by actions. A great speaker puts it best when he says, "Successful people do things consistently, what ordinary people do occasionally."

FASTING & PRAYING

Fasting can also help us prepare for a new perspective in our life. When we have a strong desire to hear from our Heavenly Father, I suggest we should sometimes have a willingness to abstain from food and certain activities. However, fasting does not mean we will get a prompt answer and that we will convince our Heavenly Father to grant us what we want. We just can't allow ourselves to be impatient and unwilling to make sacrifices of waiting. If we end up stepping ahead of God's best and not pushing through the waiting process, we suffer the consequences of using our own human knowledge and understanding and find ourselves in a self-demotion situation. However, when we anticipate hearing from the Heavenly Father, we will become better disciplined in the process of staying patient. We will have a stronger desire of drawing closer to our creator while waiting for his direction. Loving ourselves and others as a career should stay consistent, because loving ourselves and others occasionally will not bring successful results. Our own selfish behavior includes eating destructively, drinking abusively or excessive alcohol, lust, overspending, bad habits, and participating in poor and immoral behavior turns into bad character. It may seem like you have it all together at some point, but there is more substance we need to give our body that will produce our gifts and talents to be used more effectively than you fail to recognize. I know you have heard the phrase "there is more to life than what meets the eye". It is true. We should produce a relationship with our creator, we should produce love, and we should produce a genuine relationship with others. Our lives are put on this earth far more than just our pleasurable desires and what we consider fun. We are made for other purposes. Our Heavenly Father is willing and have the desire to give us a new beginning, a new look, a new makeover, a new life and a new career. The essential purpose of all is "Launching Love as Your Career." Love goes beyond telling someone those words. "I Love You." Love is expressed by action. We were invented to go beyond the call of duty called service. Stepping out of our comfort zones by helping others and giving back is love. You may be saying, I do help others. I go to a job five days a week and work 40 hours or more a day and that is all I must give. "I give what is expected of me." Which brings me to my next point. When you go to work, whether you are working for a company, or you may be an entrepreneur. How do you react when love is not being shown in the place of business? Do you allow negative words and foul language to come out of your mouth? Do you show aggressive body language when others step at you the wrong way? How do you react to people when you are at the place of worship or at the grocery store? We will be talking more about this in detail when discussing relationships. It is our responsibility as an individual to carry ourselves physically in a certain way, a loving way. I know it's not easy, and I know that your body language may not always react the way you would have hoped, but that's where launching love as your career comes into place. It starts with prayer. We are human beings, but with help of our Heavenly Father, he will lead us into consistent habits of humbleness, kindness, patience, forgiveness, and love. Make the decision to allow our father to be the one we report to and holds our future. The one that will love us unconditionally, the one we can depend on, the one whom when we make a mistake, he doesn't terminate us. The one who forgives us and cleanses us from all unrighteousness. Even when we have been driven to our sinful actions, our creator sees the potential in us and counsels us to become someone better. The one that values us, the one that will never tell your business, the one that gives us peace during difficult times, the one that heals your hurt and physical body, the one that will pay you what you are worth, and the one that will elevate you when the time is right. Our body only reacts to what we allow. I recommend we do a self-evaluation test on ourselves, not someone else. If you noticed, I said self-evaluation. Our goal should be wanting to be more like Jesus and less of ourselves. We should be striving to be faithful, committed, motivated, and willing to serve in all areas of our lives. By showing love, compassion, empathy and concern for others. These actions will allow us to focus more on others and take less focus off our problems, situations, and circumstances. It brings healing to the soul. Romans 14:19. Why would we have people make us stressful when we will be interacting with people for the rest of our lives. **Love** is limitless and beyond reach. **Love** cannot be bought. **Love** is not an emotion that you can pay for. **Love** is permanent, love endures, and love is a powerful quality to have that freely give away. Pursue love with peace, kindness, patience, selflessness, and forgiveness. Romans 12:18.

With, launching love as your career it will terminate us from feeling prideful, hostility, jealousy, frustration, worry, anxiety, and discouragement, which leads to division, violence, unforgiveness, conflicts, and a critical spirit. Giving our love, our time, and our financial contributions to help others is a gift from our Heavenly Father. When we can give to others what our Heavenly Father has given to us. That's when we know we have been blessed. We all have our own special gifts, that's why we don't have to compare ourselves to others. We just must allow our gift of love to flow into someone else so that the blessing of love will continue to be contagious. In the next chapter we will be discussing ways that we can show love to ourselves and others through our spirit.

CHAPTER 8 – THE SPIRIT

8.1 - WHAT IS A SPIRIT?

A spirit is a non-physical part of a person which shows character and emotions of the soul. This spirit needs assistance when it comes to fleshly desires. It is helpless, difficult to obey, lacks self-control and discipline while demonstrating unwise decisions.

8.2 - WHAT IS THE HOLY SPIRIT?

The Holy Spirit is a spirit of holiness that enters an unbeliever's spirit by convicting and leading the unbeliever to salvation. The holy spirit seeks to glorify Jesus Christ, Our Savior. When consistently praying and meditating on God's word, the Spirit of truth will guide our life, encourage us through faith, and transform our heart. The Holy Spirit will reinforce its power in us in order to develop Godly character through us so that we can apply Godly principles to our life.

Everyone has a spirit. Our spirit is controlled by what we input into it. Our spirit determines who we are as a person. We can choose to have a spirit of hatred, anger, jealousy, lustfulness, selfishness, pride, and greed. Another option is choosing to have a spirit of being genuine, humble, compassionate, peaceful, gentleness, meekness, hospitable, patience, and forgiving.

I'm praying that before we continue to read about the spirit, as you are considering accepting Jesus Christ as your personal savior. God's son was brought on the earth to teach us about the Heavenly Father so that one day when the world is all over or our lives have ended, we will have a place to go. A place where we can live for eternity. Right now, at this moment. I'm not talking about a sworn oath saying that you will never make mistakes, mess up, or fall short. More like taking a courageous step to say that you will be willing to live for Christ although you are not perfect. I'm not saying as you keep trying and can't seem to get it right, you will no longer be a part of God's family. Because God is a forgiving creator. (1 John 1:9). When we make up in our mind or have any type of thought of getting saved (accepting Jesus Christ as your personal savior), it's not all about us giving up smoking, drinking, sexual desires, bad attitudes, thoughtless actions, unkind speech, uncontrolled emotions, ungodly thoughts, and other sinful habits. It's about giving up your independence to our Heavenly Father and allowing his Holy Spirit to equip you to become a new person. There will be a process of transformation. A total transformation may not happen right away, but our goal should strive to be like Christ. Not only will our Heavenly Father's light shine within us but our glow will draw people closer to our Father. I'm simply offering you to be a part of God's family, the one who created us, the one who wants the best for us and the one who will love us and forgive us when no one else will. Jesus Christ, our savior is offered to every single person. (John 3:16).

Jesus came on the earth in human form, offered his service to others, and died a gruesome death just to save us from sin so that we will have a chance to live in eternity someday. Therefore, salvation is welcomed to every person that is willing to act on behalf of their own free will. If you are interested, I strongly advise that you make a heartfelt commitment on confessing that you are a sinner to our Heavenly Father. Everyone is a sinner before getting saved. Ask the Heavenly Father to come into your life and take complete control. Confess to the Lord that you believe that Jesus Christ is the only son, and he was raised from death. Once you have spoken these words with your tongue from your heart. You are saved by the grace of God. Our identity will no longer be applied as a sinner but as God's chosen sons and daughters.

We have now started the process of Launching Love as your Career. We now can focus on making progress in our life and not just rely on our human spirit, but we can rely on the wisdom of the Holy Spirit to be our leader, our teacher, our guide, and our comforter. Often, our human flesh may want to go against what the Holy Spirit equips us to do, but we must practice dependence on the Holy Spirit by obeying and trusting for our creator to do great things through us while encouraging each other to do the same. Being knowledgeable about our creator's principles and his promises will allow the Holy Spirit to live inside us and act in our creator's purpose. The Holy Spirit also helps us to be humble, joyful, peaceful, wise, and self-confident, self-controlled and submissive even during our oppositions. Our faith does not work without the Holy Spirit. Therefore, the more knowledge we acquire, the more we pray and intimately spend time with our Father, the more indestructible our faith will grow. Our spirit is led by what we read, what we watch, what we listen to, and our environment. Whether negative or positive, whatever spirit we allow in our inner circle through spoken words and our thoughts will eventually turn into our actions. Let's evaluate examples of our strengths and weaknesses for a moment.

Strengths: creative, flexible, versatile, focus on responsibilities, ability to understand other people's view, purpose driven, self-motivated, enthusiastic, go getter, mentor, leader, analyzer, organizer, peacemaker, good decision maker, not being the problem but being the solution, planner, patient, forgiving, generous, helpful, confident, compromising, manage time wisely, self-efficient, trustworthy, tenderhearted, and spending time in God's word by seeking wisdom.

Weaknesses: self-critical, insecure, judgmental, don't like to speak up for what is right, unorganized, over sensitive, don't like to adapt, envious, over thinker, bossy, unaccountable for own actions, carnal, prideful, lazy, unwilling to communicate, isolated, unmotivated, conceited, procrastination, greedy, selfish, impatient, easily annoyed, rude, and constant complaining,

8.3 - STRENGTH VS. WEAKNESS

It's always wise to look for our own strengths and weaknesses so that we can learn about ourselves and hopefully be willing to make changes in areas that can be improved. We cannot overcome our adversities without the references of our Heavenly Father and the Holy Spirit to guide us. The Holy Spirit qualifies us with the strength and the ability to be skilled at living a rewarding life. You may feel that you are in control. It's only the deception of the enemy that makes you want to feel like you can make it on your own. We try to achieve happiness by striving after our own desires, realizing later that we are tired and unsatisfied. When we rely on the Holy Spirit to help us with his wisdom, strength, and courage, we can strive to eliminate bad habits. Strive to leave an unhealthy relationship. Strive to have peace during a difficult situation. Strive to speak victory over our body when the doctors have said there is no hope. Strive to forgive even when haven't been forgiven by others. Strive to love and strive to take the necessary steps to emerge from our comfort zone. We should ask the Holy Spirit to strengthen us through faith. James 2:17 is stated "faith without works is dead." Wisdom to know that when we are facing hardship, our loving father hasn't forgotten us, but we are reminded that there is a divine purpose in the midpoint of our career development. Our creator tests our faith while producing endurance and maturity in our life. He wants us to grow and utilize the resources throughout our daily life in order to embrace our strength and courage of learning God's word and focusing on his promises.

HAVING FAITH V/S. TAKING RISKS

Let me narrate a very interesting story I believe to be worth sharing. One of the things I learned during this whole entire experience was, "if you believe in whatever you are selling including the value of yourself, you can sell it!" I was driving in my car one day. Suddenly an idea came to my mind. I will humbly give God the credit of sending the Holy Spirit my way. It had to be because this idea I know within my own nature. I would have never thought of doing anything remotely out of the norm and thinking outside of my own comfort zone box. "The idea of selling my mother's cake!" My mother was an extraordinary woman. She raised six girls, worked multiple jobs, and she had a talent for baking cakes. I knew my mother's cakes were the bomb because people would always brag on them, and she would have tons of cake orders during the holidays. So, a light bulb came on like, "Why don't I have my mom to bake whole cakes, slice them and I would go around in different areas and sell each slice."

I was already in the process of thinking of ways of making extra money. I ran the idea by my mom and sold her on the idea. I'm not going to sugarcoat it. I was afraid, but not to the point of not trying it. I even ran my idea across to a coworker and received a negative response. She was like, "no one is going to buy cakes because people are trying to lose weight." Another thing I learned on this journey; you cannot let everyone know your ideas because it can discourage you. Secondly, just because it didn't work for someone else, doesn't mean it won't work for you. Especially if it's in your heart to do. I believe the cake idea was in my heart to do because I didn't get discouraged, I was just in a little doubt and fear, which are natural emotions. Basically, I didn't allow my coworker's negative input to stop me from doing what was in me to do. I suggest that you only talk to those that you know have your best interests and after prayer, you must step into faith.**" Hebrews 11:1"** or take the risks of uncertainty. I love this book of John Maxwell when he talks about growth. He says, "when we take risks, sometimes we fail, and sometimes we succeed, but we are always learning." But when we allow faith to guide us through what we are not certain about, we can be assured about things that we hope for even when it hasn't yet been seen. The first day of selling my mom's cakes, I will never forget it. I walked into a hair salon. I was already thinking, what am I going to say? So, my line was, "Would anyone like to purchase a lemon pound cake, sour cream pound cake, red velvet cake and etc.?" The first response was no. Then, I went to a place next door and said the same exact thing. Guess what? One person said no, but the other person said yes! "I would like to buy a slice, how much?" I was selling each slice of cake for $2.50 each. I felt so encouraged after that moment, and then it was on like the popcorn seeds in a microwave. My selling slices of cakes started "popping." I would even get people to taste the cake and I would say, "If you don't like it, you don't have to buy it. Of course, they were buying it every time. I even had issues sometimes with owners asking me not to solicit in their establishment. What I would do is offer them a complimentary slice of cake, and they would allow me to sell to their customers. Wow! Most times you can get away with things when you show good customer service skills. My mom's cakes became popular in hair salons, barbershops, and people started flagging me down on the streets through word of mouth. I literally became known as the "Cake Lady." Even mom's brownies became a hit! During the holidays, my customers would order a whole cake. I would give my mom a profit for her baking, but her beautiful spirit did it to help me out. Sadly, to say after a couple of years passed, mom got overwhelmed with orders. She was already up in age. She said she was ready to stop because she felt like it was getting too dangerous for me to be on the streets. Maybe it was some truth to that and then also I'm sure she was tired too and didn't want to let me down. This was my having faith v/s taking a risk moment. I was able to succeed at it and reach my potential that I didn't know that I had. By believing in my potential and stepping out of my comfort zone. I did the leg work, but God gave me the courage to overcome my fear and doubt. He believed in me before I believed in myself. With the right mindset and a realistic agenda, God gives us the ability and opportunities to see the value within ourselves so that you can "Launch Love as Your Career."

CHAPTER 9 – THE TRAINING GUIDE

9.1 - LAUNCHING LOVE AS YOUR CAREER TRAINING GUIDE

A training guide is a list of instructions to guide us through the process of improving the quality of the way we live. It is to give us guidelines to follow so that we can stay on track and be able to perform our daily tasks in order to produce the best results. Without the essentials of knowing what is required of us in order to live a healthy lifestyle, it's impossible to launch love as your career. Look at some of the most important qualities to have and what not to have when we are constantly moving towards our journey.

Have Love

Love cannot be bought. It goes beyond human visibility and deepens far more than human definition. Our loving Father's Love is perfect, unconditional, trustworthy, and never changes. His Love forgives. Having a heart for our creator is a valuable goal to achieve. We will never be perfect, but when we consistently advance in a relationship with our Heavenly Father, we will begin to aim towards the desires and interests that are pleasing to him. By doing so, we ultimately create Love for others.

Have Humility

Humbleness is demonstrated when our fleshly habits and thoughts become under submission through the Holy Spirit. By educating ourselves with our Heavenly Father's biblical knowledge and his words of wisdom will become useful in our daily lives. We will be taught, trained, and corrected into righteous living. The whole idea of humility is not to depend on ourselves but to surrender and allow the Holy Spirit to indwell in us.

Have Compassion

Sympathy and concern for others can be obtained when our minds are renewed through our Heavenly Father's words. When we make an effort to seek after and focus on the purpose Our Creator has prepared for us, we can then eliminate being self-centered and start centering our attention on others. Our Father has gifted us with the ability, and the resources, to demonstrate compassion towards others. Ask yourself if you are willing to be selfless and inconvenienced when giving up your personal time? Are we willing to make ourselves available to others when others are in need? Are we at an arm's length and can be found accessible in such circumstances? Once we draw closer to our Father's Love and obedience, we will achieve a heart of compassion towards others through our thoughts and actions.

Ephesians 4:32

Have Empathy

Understanding the feelings of others is essential. It's easy to be kind to others when others are nice to us. However, it's more demanding of us to respond to unkindness with Love. But we must do it anyway because we're asked to do so. Jesus Christ, our Father's son, performed a great example of empathy when he sacrificed his life on the cross to save us from our sins so that we may have a rewarding life. Certainly, we can be grateful enough to rely on the Holy Spirit's strength to enable God's divine Love to flow through us and into others. Our Heavenly Father is pleased with us when we express Love for one another. Even though God's unconditional Love is not standard in our society, others will take notice when they see Love is demonstrated in us. Have you ever heard of the "Golden Rule"? It tells us to treat others as we would want to be treated. When we have mastered this rule with the help of the Holy Spirit, relationships become more important and of greater value. When we rely on the importance of healthy relationships, we become more understanding and more willing to help each other. Without loving relationships, life falls short of purpose and meaning. There is not much to look forward to in life without meaningful relationships, and life becomes very lonely and disconnected.

Have Peace

Serenity and peace are established to exist when we start having a personal relationship with our Heavenly Father. Our creator asks us to "cast our burdens on him, and he will sustain us" Psalms 55:22. He may not take away all the difficulties that we face in life, but he will take the weight of worry, frustration, doubt, confusion, hopelessness and place it in his own hands. He will give us peace when we put our confidence, reliance, trust, hope, and faith in Him. When we pray about our trials, challenges, difficulties and adversities, we should seek his guidance and quote his promises so that we can experience his faithfulness towards us.

Have Gentleness

This word is not often used, but it brings about kindness which is sometimes a struggle to express due to the reason of how broken the world is. The different types of people we encounter are often eye-opening. When we consistently meditate on our Heavenly Father's word in Galatians 5:22, we can replace pride with humbleness and compassion for others. Oftentimes, we can't focus on how we are handled but how we are to handle the situation that will be well pleasing to God.

Have Meekness

Being submissive isn't about being powerless or weak. It's about knowing who is on our side and who will fight our battles. "2 Chronicles 20:15." Our Heavenly Father created us; He didn't create any of us to be powerless. Our creator sent the Holy Spirit to indwell in us so that we can have enough power over the enemy. Not through cruelty to others, harsh words, and violence, but through submission to the Heavenly Father. He empowers us through his words that we don't have to be always physically strong but being mentally strong is just as powerful.

Have Genuineness

Realness, authenticity, and originality are often expressed through our character, conduct, and conversation. Not just these three things, but through our skills, talents and gifts. The more we pursue our Heavenly Father's lifestyle, the less we would want to chase and tolerate wrongdoings in today's culture. Once we indulge in worship and praise towards our Heavenly Father, we will begin to see that our priorities and attitudes begin to change. Genuine success is innovated through our responsibility on earth while accomplishing the goals that our creator sets for us through our personality, talents, abilities, and spiritual gifts. If we live by our creator's definition of success, our life on earth will be pleasing, satisfying, fulfilling, edifying, and beneficial. No matter how gifted, talented, skillful or successful we are on earth, God utilizes us to glorify himself. When our life is over on this earth and I'm hoping that we are or become saved and make it to heaven. We will receive the greatest reward of all. And it will be all worth the wait and anticipation.

Have Patience

Patience means to tolerate everything without getting quickly upset or angry and to obediently endure and preserve your challenges. It requires not rushing into making decisions without talking it over with the Holy Spirit. While trusting, praying, and having faith in our Father, we can expect to be favored and hear his voice by waiting on God to see us through. Isaiah 40:31. While we are in the process of putting our skills into practice on this earth, love with patience. We are provided with opportunities to care, listen, understand, and serve others with patience.

Have Forgiveness

Forgiveness means being competent of not holding a grudge against someone. An essential part of forgiveness is healing. Forgiveness heals the mind, the heart, the spirit, and relationships. Without forgiveness, it causes sickness in our bodies. If we don't adopt a habit of forgiveness, it causes division and conflict towards others. And the worst of all, it causes a distant relationship with the Heavenly Father. The reason why it causes a distant relationship with the Heavenly Father is that our Heavenly Father says that "Vengeance is His" Hebrews 10:30. According to his words, we must leave the judging and punishment to Him. Forgiveness does not mean that we must continue a close relationship like it once was, or we won't be hurt emotionally by someone that has hurt us or has hurt someone we love. However, when we are willing to be dependent on the Holy Spirit, we can then pray through our bitterness, anger, and hurt to our creator. Our creator will then act on our behalf.

Have Hospitality

Being hospitable means being welcoming and friendly to others. If you read John 13:14 & 15 in the Bible, our Heavenly Father gives us an example of how his son Jesus Christ performed one of the most distasteful but humble acts of service by washing people's dirty feet. Jesus came on earth to be an example to the world. Jesus wants us to realize that every task that we are assigned is important to our Father's kingdom. Jesus gives us the aspiration to be willing to serve others with a positive attitude and a loving heart. Jesus desires for us to do away with pride, selfishness, positions, greed and power. Once we become the way Jesus wants us to be, we should be willing to give our time, resources and assist those who are in need of it.

Have Hope, Peace & Joy

Hope means knowing God will make a way while peace is waiting in the process, and joy is a strong feeling of contentment while waiting in the process of God demonstrating his course of action. Giving unto God, we as followers of Jesus Christ should choose to live with a compassionate heart and sacrificial spirit while increasing our faith in God. We have the assurance of knowing that our creator will supply us with enough to meet all of our needs. Philippians 4:19

Have Not Hatred

Hatred is an intense dislike towards someone or something. It can start with your upbringing: depending on what you were taught and what your environment was like. If we have a hard time dealing with our hurts, it develops a feeling of hatred within us. Instead of praying and taking our hurts to our Heavenly Father or even a trustworthy friend, we may choose negative methods and give in to the hatred within us. We rehearse the pain in our mind by allowing resentment in our hearts, and then bitterness grows into our spirit, causing negative emotions, attitudes, and sometimes our physical health is challenged. When we experience hatred in our hearts, it puts up barriers which terminates the ability to love others and receive Love from others.

Have Not Jealousy

Jealousy is a feeling of envy. Jealousy is often an overwhelming feeling of insecurity we often face due to others or our circumstances. In order to get rid of this emotion in our life, we must be honest with ourselves and our almighty Father that we feel this way about someone or something. The first step is to acknowledge that you're feeling a certain way before looking at ways of how to eradicate them. It will be difficult to have a loving relationship with our Father when there is a jealousy spirit. Although jealousy is common, it is also unhealthy. Jealousy leads to comparing our life's success with someone else's success and builds up an unhealthy desire of wanting what may not be meant for us. It can place fear in our spirit that we may lose what we already have. Due to jealousy, we may feel that we can never have enough or even been enough. You will experience a lack of peace because someone else's success becomes a constant distraction for you. If we pray and ask our creator for his best for us and be grateful for our talents, gifts, and abilities that we have received so far in our lives, we won't have to face the need to compare our lives to others. We can experience a joyful and satisfying lifestyle if we choose to eradicate the feeling of jealousy from its root cause.

Have Not Anger

Anger includes intense emotions. This emotion starts off when we experience sudden threats, insults, injustices, anxieties, and frustrations. This emotion turns into resentment, which in result is poisoning our thinking. When we allow this ruthless emotion to take authority over our spirit, it shows up in our behavior. This behavior then provokes us into enmity that is an act of being hostile to someone. Anger destroys our joy and peace.

Have Not Dissension

Dissension is a disagreement that leads to conflict and antagonism. This behavior puts us into a position of acting with hostility. These behaviors can destroy our character, relationships with others, and ultimately, our relationship with our Heavenly Father. Arguments tears down our spirit of calmness and serenity and take it up to a spirit level of being out of order with chaos. Our spirit can become super contagious to others and even trigger down to future generations. Maintaining our disagreements through the empowerment of the Holy Spirit keeps us from stress, brokenness, resentment, and hostility.

Have Not Lustfulness

Strong sexual desires are increasing day by day. We all have had strong desires that can leave us feeling powerless. That's a part of our human nature. However, it is also a form of sin. When we see ourselves falling into the trap of lustfulness, we can pray and ask the Holy Spirit to guard our hearts and mind against it. Instead of indulging in sinful behavior, we must pray and ask God to deliver us from our foolish ways.

Have Not Selfishness

Selfishness is showing excessive concern for oneself. When you see a selfish person, they normally want things their way, and they want it right away. They are not willing to wait. They are more concerned about themselves than others. This feeling develops immense negativity and superficial desires.

Have Not Greed

Greed is an intense desire for wealth, material possessions, fame, and power, even if it means to lie, cheat, steal, and kill to get what we want. In order to get rid of this ungrateful behavior, we must develop intentional habits within ourselves in order to increase our generosity towards others.

Have Not Pride

Lovers of themselves, feeling superior or better than others. Portraying yourself falsely on social media and other social platforms in order to be admired falls under pride. Relying on our own strength, wisdom, and abilities when we want to determine our own destiny is what makes one full of pride too.

9.2 - PARTICIPATING IN THE MIDST OF ADVERSITY WHILE GLORIFYING GOD IN THE PROCESS

When facing the evil spirits of our enemy, there are times we will encounter adversity. Adversity is when trouble and difficulties will affect us mentally, emotionally, socially, spiritually, and even financially throughout our lives. Jesus told us that we would have troubles, but during this time, we shall have peace and be of good cheer because he has overcome the world. John 16:33. I also like the quote that says, "Success is to be measured not so much by the position that one has reached in life, but by the obstacles which one has overcome,"

Adversity will be a part of your life. It cannot be avoided. It may be a marriage that is falling apart, children that are heading in the opposite direction of God's direction. Trouble on the job, a difficult family member or friend you can't get along with, churchs showing division, health issues, mental issues, or money issues. Whatever it is that's causing us to be worried, stressed out, frustrated, confused, and anxious is considered as adversity. Adversity happens, but it's the way you handle it when it comes our way. That is why it is wise to depend on the Holy Spirit. The Holy Spirit supplies everything we need to live a successful life when we place our faith, hope, and trust in our Heavenly Father. The Holy Spirit's purpose is to strengthen us with God's power during our adversity. Proverbs 24:10.

Another way for us to find strength in adversity is by looking at our situation from God's perspective, through reading his word. If we don't study and get the knowledge and the truth, we need to overcome the lies of the enemy we will not have the ability, skills, qualifications and resources that we need to fight off our enemy. Proverbs 24:10, 2 Timothy 2:15, and James 1:5.

It may be questionable for us to believe that our Heavenly Father loves us because of what we go through. We must ask the Holy Spirit to show us what God wants us to see from his view. Then we must look at our opposition as God's opportunity to help us to grow, all while depending on God increases our faith and hope in him. Often times we are doing what we want to do by pleasing ourselves and end up in a mess of trouble. We even make unhealthy decisions, yet we are forgiven by his grace. However, if we don't see God's way, we possibly won't make it out of a bad situation. Every negative experience and evil spirit that continues to live inside us will bring our body to sickness and possibly death. We start off with a psychological war in our mind, and then we find ourselves battling a war in our spirit. The enemy is going to throw everything he can at us to discourage us. The enemy will even demand our character. One of the quotes that caught my attention was, "Watch your thoughts that lead to attitude. Watch your attitude that leads to words. Watch your words that lead to action. Watch your actions that lead to habits. Watch your habits that form your character. Watch your character, which then determines your destiny."

The enemy's evil spirit will try to oppress us with strife, conflict, stress, bitterness, hate, confusion, frustration, envy, intimidation, unworthiness, inadequacy, discouragement, worry, fear, guilt, jealousy, and pride. The enemy wants to steal our faith, hope, and joy. The enemy wants to kill our dreams, and the enemy wants to destroy our destiny. **John 10:10** states that **the enemy "comes to steal, kill and destroy."** The enemy wants us to doubt the promises of God. The enemy wants us to quit and give up. Galatians 6:9.

Whenever there is a challenge in our situation, there are distractions designed for the enemy to move us away or terminate us from our destiny.

One of my admirers in the Bible was the apostle Paul. He was a great Christian leader. Why? Because Paul was imprisoned and served for quite a period of jail time. During this time in his life, he was experiencing adversity. Something great came out of Paul's hardship. Paul had the courage to speak and minister to those who He encountered with. The help of the Holy Spirit, providing him with mental and physical stamina. Paul had become an effective servant. Paul allowed the Holy Spirit to release its power through him for the purpose of our Father's will to be fulfilled. The apostle Paul relied upon the strength of the Father by staying faithful and never giving up. (2 Corinthians 12:9) says, "My grace is sufficient for you, for power is perfected in weakness."

I have great news! On the way to accomplishing the goals, the purpose, the destiny, and God's will for our lives. There will be risks worth taking vs. faith worth having. The Holy Spirit will qualify us to have the courage to preserver. Our Heavenly Father is aware that sometimes we will become weak, tired, and hopeless, but he asks us to rely on his strength and not our own. We then will be able to achieve our self-value and carry out our daily tasks by being positive, motivated, inspired, dedicated, committed, consistent, and determined with life's journey. We will be empowered to use God's weapon in his words and not feel the pressure of worldly weapons. Let's allow God to do good work in us. Philippians 1:6. Let's allow God to supernaturally restart your heart so that you can launch Love As your Career.

CHAPTER 10 – SPIRITUAL RESUME PROFILE

A spiritual resume is a summary and a list of personal data that highlights our background, our training, our experiences, our qualifications and our achievements. Our spiritual resume should be an essential way to advertise, market and elevate ourselves into striving to become better human beings. By looking at some of the examples below, hopefully we can make a difference in ourselves and in the lives of others. In order to be successful and to become the right candidate that sets us apart in our position in life. One must show themselves approved amongst our Heavenly Father which are in Heaven. (2 Timothy 2:15)

Born as a worldly sinner, relying on my own independence. Sometimes, I allow my selfish ways to get the best of me. I do love my family and friends, but not so much those that I don't know and who are different than me. I know the scriptures in the Bible, but I don't have a personal relationship with the Heavenly Father. I feel like I'm a good decent person, but every now and then, I like to get out of character. I participate in contributing good deeds towards others, but I'm not born again. I'm thankful and grateful but only when things are going well. I like to pray, for only myself and for I want. I enjoy being a leader, but I don't like to be led. I like to help others, but only when it is convenient for me.

Work History

*Fed the hungry at the homeless shelter

*Distributed food to those in need

*Oversee strategic projects for the youth ministry

*Served on the committee of administering clothes to the less fortunate

*Circulated assistance to senior citizens who are not capable to do for themselves.

Experience

*Assisted others that are in need

*Utilize praise and worship as a way of honoring the creator

*Pray through adversity without ceasing

*Meditate on God's words to gain wisdom

*Demonstrate love through actions

Special Skills/Strengths

*Empower others

*A prayer warrior

*Embracing change

*Strive for peace when going through a storm

*Demonstrating kindness with no hidden intentions

*The awareness of knowing that I can do all things through Christ who strengthens me

Weakness

*A feeling of being overlooked when I haven't heard from God

*Being disobedient to the spirit when I want things my way

*Being critical or judge mental towards others

*Gossiping

*Following human flesh desires

Awards/Achievements

*Accepting Jesus Christ as my personal savior and now my name is written in the book of life.

*A disciple of God for many years

*Blessed financially

*Great abundance of health

*Beautiful healthy and humble children

*I'm not a hater, I'm a congratulator

*I love not only my family and friends; I love all those who God has created

*I may sometimes get disappointed but not angry when things don't follow my plans

*I have matured to learn patience and wait on God's timing by applying his promises to my life daily

Education

*Bible

*Concordance

*Audio/CD

*Authors books about the Bible

*Sunday School

References

The Holy Bible, KJV, NIV, Podcast,

What is your spiritual resume?

CHAPTER 11 – LOVE AT EVERY ANGLE

Relationships: the way in which two or more people stay connected.

There are many different areas of relationships. The importance of a healthy relationship requires respect, patience, forgiveness, and Love not only for yourself but for others. It's an investment that will carry you throughout your entire life.

We all know that there is a thing, such as bad relationships. We must be able to distinguish between the negative ones as opposed to the positive ones. Some people think their security lies in other people, their own bank accounts, their prestige, and their possessions. This can lead to becoming a workaholic, someone who is willing to sacrifice their relationships for financial gain. We are sometimes tempted into engaging in unethical activities. We may even search for excitement in an inappropriate relationship which can lead to pain and disappointment. It pleases the enemy to depend on ourselves so that we become out of line with our Heavenly Father's will. This type of wrong thinking will direct our actions and cause us to get into difficult situations.

Relationships go beyond who we may know, who we may like, what someone can do for us. For many relationships, relationships have a motive. In this chapter, we will talk about God first, ourselves, spouses, children, parents (the elderly), family members, coworkers, acquaintances, relational friends, guests, clients, customers, and unexpected encounters.

Hopefully, by the time you have made it to the last chapter of this book, you have now made up your mind about becoming saved, or you are taking the steps towards rededicating your life back to the Lord whom created you. However, if you have not, I will continue to pray that every person reading this book will become saved, and then Launching Love as your Career will become a part of your life. Even though times may get rough, times may be challenging, times may be unfair, times may be unjust, times may seem overwhelming, times may seem unpredictable, times may seem inconsistent, times may seem out of order; all and all, launching Love as your Career will start out as your goal, which can hopefully then position you into your destiny.

11.1 - LOVING GOD

When accepting Jesus Christ as our personal savior, everyone has the chance to have a fresh new start in life. We all were born into the sin of a broken world. Through our faith in Jesus and the grace of our Heavenly Father, we can receive forgiveness if we ask and start over as new beings in Christ. We talked about the spirit earlier therefore, we must invite the Holy Spirit to dwell in us as well. Having a relationship with God is like having any other relationship. When we give our hearts the permission to fall in Love with Jesus, we are eager to express a contagious joy within. When we spend time with the holy spirit, we talk to the holy spirit, we think about the holy spirit, we pray in the holy spirit, these actions will lead us into the divine meditation of the holy spirit guiding us. We are then able to share our Love with others. For those that may not ever have had an encounter with God, it may seem unfamiliar or even foreign being in tune with the holy spirit, but the more you spend time in all areas of your relationship with God, your discernment will become profound and it will feel natural. There may be times when it seems like we don't feel God, but he's always in our presence.

Let's talk about evil spirits for a moment. You may not believe in them, but they are very much real, just like the spirit of God. If there weren't any evil spirits, why do you think there are diseases, violence, murder, greed, hate, the Love of material things, and worldly possessions even to mention the stronghold of cigarettes, drugs, alcohol, gambling, and sexual immorality that exists? We all were created by God no matter what color we are and where we come from. It's challenging at times to love someone that doesn't love us back. Those we may not know personally, those that treat us unfairly, those that are jealous, those that hate, those that do spiteful things, those that condescendingly talk to you, those that judge you based on their own opinions. Regardless of any negative experiences that we have faced with others, it does not justify us not to love them and meaning others for harm. God said, "we are to love others despite the fact that we live in a world that's filled with darkness, we can shine our light with the influence of righteous behavior." (Matthew 5:16). Being led by this example, we may be able to lead someone the way to Jesus Christ. Jesus wants us to serve one another with humility and Love. God wants us to see ourselves as living sacrifices and value to the world. Our responsibility is not to judge and condemn others, but it is our responsibility to pray for them. It does require us to meditate on God's words, chew on God's words and digest in our spirit for us to become successful at loving those that are not so loving. It's not up to us to decide who we are going to love. The goal is to pursue love like it's your Career.

11.2 - LOVING OURSELVES

Loving yourself is very important. We live in a world that has a motive for everything. If you do for me, then I will do it for you. If you don't love yourself completely, how do you know what is good for you and what is not? That's why it is very wise not to compare yourselves to others. It is a very dangerous road to follow. We all know that everyone is different. Whether it's someone's culture, race, weight, height, body structure, hair, eye color, or personality. There is probably something about all of us that we would like to change. However, we should also look in the mirror and find good qualities about ourselves. There is a negative spirit out there that will tell us that we don't look better, we don't have better, we don't perform better. A feeling of being inadequate to others that is just a lie from the enemy because God made us specifically for his purpose and who he wants us to be. God is a perfect God, so why didn't he just create us to be the same? It's nothing wrong when we can go online and see something we like or read something we like about a person that we admire, which I mentioned previously. I suggest then that we allow that person or persons we admire to inspire us to be the best person we are created to be, which makes us unique. Others then will see the natural us, the authentic us, the original us and the one and only us. We can then launch Love as our Career.

11.3 - LOVING YOUR SPOUSE

Loving your spouse or your mate or your partner or your special friend, whichever one relates to you. Especially in the beginning, the relationship feels so wonderful, so fulfilling, so special, doesn't it? It's a great feeling to love someone, and it's even an awesome more feeling of being in Love with someone. Those that can relate know that feelings change. We base our Love on what someone does for us, how someone makes us feel or what things we have in common. We feel at the time that we can spend the rest of our lives together. Through certain circumstances, we get to the point that situations change. People change. People become different after time. Couples may get to the point of wanting a new partner for whatever reason. Couples outgrow each other. Couples may not respect the other person as they should. Couples may decide they are going in a different direction than they were before. The money has gotten funny. All these can be a factor in breaking up, but it doesn't mean we can't continue to love. I know you may be saying to me while reading this portion of the book that I just don't understand what the person in your life has done to you. You are absolutely correct. I don't know. I do know what will help you to move your life to a more stressless and victorious life. I would suggest to anyone when you decide to leave or the other person decides to leave, or both parties agree to depart, please forgive one another. Circumstances are different when you are married. I don't want any Christians or believers to beat me down by saying married people are not to get a divorce or married couples shouldn't seek counseling first. I do agree with that, I would suggest taking all necessary actions first to try saving your marriage. This book is not geared towards counseling on marriage; this book is about maintaining a healthy lifestyle so that we can launch Love as our Career in the process of being joyful, peaceful, and loved in our relationships.

11.4 - LOVING YOUR CHILDREN

Children are a very important part of our lives. They are the future. They are where we used to be. Now they are making their way to become adults. When I was writing this book, I did not have a certain age, sex, color, or even gender in mind. I hope that this book can reach anyone that will be willing to read it, share it and encourage those that we encounter. My prayer is that we would allow our Love to be manifested into our children and other's children by teaching them how to become mature spiritual men and women. We can start by showing them how much we appreciate them and teaching them that God values them as well. If we want the best results in our children, we must be willing to be good examples. One of the essential ways of being an example to our children is by demonstrating Godly character. Which we will talk about in more detail concerning parents. It's sad if we feel that we always must try to make our children comfortable and giving them their way is the best way to earn their respect in order for them to obey us and see us as great leaders. This is farther from the truth. Biblical principles are the guide that will impact and equip the next generation to start a relationship with their creator, themselves, and others. It will help them learn what the plan for their life is through our Heavenly Father's eyes. It will assist them with their choices while being held accountable for their decision-making and aid them through having a disciplined heart. I know there are some of us that haven't had kids, but we all can be an example in different areas. Some of us are aunts and uncles, cousins, stepparents, educators, pastors, mentors, counselors, big brothers, big sisters, and Sunday school teachers. I was reading somewhere that mentioned, raising a child without a biblical foundation is like sending them to war without weapons and armor. As an adult and younger adult, we will always be put in a position to be an example to someone else. I'm not asking you to become a parent to someone else's child but look for an opportunity to mentor a child through activity involvements, reading together, communicating to them about their thoughts, their interests, what makes them joyful, what bothers them, and listening to what is important to them. Teach children right from wrong and show them unconditional love even when we know they are wrong and being mischievous. Mentoring is about taking time to share our knowledge, wisdom, skills, talents, and gifts. Giving children our hugs, telling them we love them, sharing with them that we all make mistakes, and how to recover once mistakes have been made. We are to forgive them even though they choose not to obey at the time. Being patient with them when they don't seem to understand things as fast as we would want them to. Love them when they make unexcused choices. Don't these scenarios seem so familiar? These are not just situations that we were in when we were children. These are also things we do even now as adults. However, demonstrating godly influence on our children will create discipline and self-control in them.   God's grace is sufficient. Even when I'm not listening, even when I foolishly choose to make my own decisions. God is with me, not because I deserve it but because he loves me and gives me chances to make it right through his grace and mercy. If God can do that for me, why can't I find it in my heart to do the same? Children are our investment. Children are everyone's responsibility. I'm not saying that we have the right to raise other children the way we have been taught or take matters into our own hands. I am saying that sharing our Love and praying for them in place of judging them can bring on a change. I realize there are challenging times right now. Things have changed. Things are not what they used to be, but we serve a God that has not changed and never will he change. It's not about us controlling our situations, but it's about us knowing who is in control. I remember when growing up, my sisters and I had parents that believed in a spiritual foundation. We was taught to learn about our Heavenly Father at an early age. We also had Church Leaders and neighbors looking out for us. We had leaders and mentors that loved us enough to see a bigger picture. They didn't see us as someone else's responsibility. They saw us as one day growing up and becoming an adult that will be essential to the world that can make a positive difference. I know you may not see every child that way, but who are we to choose. Every child must be empowered not on our level but their level.

11.5 - LOVING YOUR PARENTS

Parents are so great to have. I have empathy for those reading this book that doesn't feel the same way I do. I had two of the greatest parents, and they were a positive influence on my life. They made sure that we had a relationship with God. We were forced to go to church which is very different nowadays. Children get to tell their parents if they want to go to church. When I see the effort my parents put forth in order to instill values in my siblings and me, I can truly say it was well worth it. Children now grow up treating and talking to their parents in a disrespectful way. God says, "Train up a child in the way they shall go, and then when they leave you, they will not go astray." (Proverbs 22:6). Training a child must start in the very beginning. God loved us before we were even created. Our children should be shown Love from the very beginning. I know in some situation this hasn't happened for some children. that this is the reason why we can't always blame children and even adults for their behavior. Training children with our Love should be demonstrated throughout their life. We can launch Love as our Career by looking for opportunities to teach them spiritual habits and values in order to exhibit righteousness towards our creator, us as parents, and others that are in authority. Loving your parents should not be based on what your parents can give you through worldly pleasures. Most of us was blessed to have parents as our caregivers and we have the same responsibility to take-care of our parents. When you focus your attention on how the world is, a lot of things that we are willing to give our kids are worldly things. We will make the mistake of giving them things that will not stay with them for the rest of their lives. instead of providing them with the necessities that will last forever. They will only get confused and find themselves searching for a dead-end career that will lead them into a dead-end situation. If we focus on demonstrating faith, humility, empathy, selflessness, patience, forgiveness, and LOVE! These attributes will lead to proper guidance for our children and generation to come. Taking care of our parents and seniors will hopefully influence our children to do the same. Who does not want to be taken care of or seen about when they are no longer able to be on their own? No one wants to hear the reality of this, but if you keep living, your time will come. These things must come to mind when you are caring for your children and inculcating values into your children. If there are teenagers reading this book, keep in mind that having a baby is more than a lifestyle, it's a lifelong commitment of becoming loving parents.

11.6 - LOVING YOUR FAMILY AND CHURCH

I put these two together because they both work in the same way. Our church family is just as important as our personal families. Why? When we are in unity with one another, our Heavenly Father honors and favors the relationship. You can tell when a team is on one accord and when they are not. When a group of people is not working together towards the same goal, there can be division and conflict. When a group of people is willing to work together for the good of the purpose, we can get things accomplished. When nourishing and maturing in relationships, we must humble ourselves by making self-sacrifices and submitted to the Holy Spirit. We all were created differently, with different assignments but for the same purpose. We have different personalities, different opinions, different gifts and talents, different backgrounds, and different characters. Some of us, if not most of us, try to function independently and selfishly. However, our creator didn't intend for it to be that way. Our creator is pleased when we work together and love one another genuinely. There are many times, if not all the time, there will be those in need, hopeless, lonely, and feeling empty, and we must stay focused so that we are prepared to accept the tasks of giving people hope in Jesus and encouragement. There will be times when we may disagree, but it's through our willingness and faithfulness to our creator to be available for others, compromising in disputes, forgiving when we've been wronged, and having a love of the Heavenly Father in us for the good of his purpose to be achieved.

11.7 - LOVING YOUR COWORKERS

Oftentimes we are unaware that we are separating our work life from our spiritual life. We should look wisely to involve our creator every day and everywhere we go. Our workplace should also be a place of ministry. Although it may not seem that we have the greatest skills and experience as someone else, we as believers should be acknowledged by doing quality work and service unto the Heavenly Father. We should be respectful to others while relying on the Holy Spirit to help us from becoming discouraged when doing what is right and pleasing to God. The workforce may be a benefit of earning a paycheck, but our spiritual benefit will motivate us to earn a reward of favor and blessings from our Father. We, as believers in the workplace, should be issuing out our responsibilities and tasks with the expression of love. Along with a servant attitude, respect towards others, and integrity. Whether it's our coworkers or our colleagues, we all have essential positions in the workforce. You could be the CEO, the President, General Manager, Director, Manager, Supervisor, Team Leader, or Employee. Even an entrepreneur. We need each other. Everyone has a role. It's up to each one of us to launch Love as Your Career in the place where we are working. You may be at a place in your life where you are not satisfied and have no peace. Have you ever looked around and discovered that it's not always the people we work around, but it could possibly be you? I know we all have challenges with something or someone. Instead of complaining and placing the blame on someone else, we must sometimes take a step back, go look into the mirror, assess ourselves and then pray on where the problem could be coming from. I'm a strong believer in not being the person to talk about the problem. I believe to be the person to acknowledge that there is a problem and where there is a problem, there is a chance to solve it. Ponder on what I said. We should not dwell on who or what is the problem but for acknowledging that there needs to be a solution. This can be helpful. There comes a time when the solution is to remove the situation from your life, or you must decide to be removed from the situation. I know you may have heard the saying "it's how you handle the situation, and it's the approach behind it". This is true. Would you rather for someone to demand something of you, or would you rather for them to ask you? Which one would sound better? Asking, right? We all have different personalities, different talents, different gifts, and different opinions, but at the end of it all, when we are working in the same space, hopefully, we all should have the same goal with a different destiny. Meaning that we all should be providing that company or our company with what we have been hired for. If you are an entrepreneur, you are hiring workers for your goal of what you want to accomplish. Suppose the people you hire are not providing the service or the product of what you need, what will be the point of having them there? Even though we may work for the same goals of the company, our destiny will be different. Why? Because we are all different with different situations and we have different responsibilities, and we are seeking to do different things in our life. Some people want to grow to gain higher positions and make more money. There are others that are comfortable where they are and prefer to just make money to take care of their families until retirement. Nothing is wrong with any scenarios, but it's how we get there together to complete our destiny. No one has control over your destiny but the Heavenly Father, our creator. That is why you cannot let coworkers and bosses stop you from where you are trying to go by showing selfishness, disrespect, ungratefulness, malice, hatred, and pride. "Love your neighbor, as you do yourself." We may not always be treated in the manner that we deserve, but good always outweighs the bad. There were many times on my job that I felt to be overlooked, being mistreated, and unfair, but God always had his hand in it. There were times I had to dismiss myself from my work area for a while just to get away from negativity and pray. I didn't understand why it always had to be me that seemed that I was giving in, but it was God giving me a sense of meekness and humbleness. Humbleness to Love others despite of and meekness of showing submissiveness to those that were in charge. I had to realize that I was not being weak. I was being wise. I assure you if you let God fight your battles, he will do it! This will not always be easy. That's why praying before we even go out of our house will be suggested because we don't know what spirit we will have to encounter. You will not always be in a place of comfortability or familiarity. My advice is never to leave a place because we are uncomfortable and can't always get our way. Being uncomfortable helps us to become discipline and adaptable. Being in a place that we can't always get our way help us to become resilient. Make an attitude adjustment because you want to grow, and you want to continue to launch Love as your Career.

Whether it's a guest, customer, client, or unexpected encounter, we are God's creation. I've mentioned before that we all were put on this earth for a purpose. The difference is that we all are different. We may sometimes have the same gifts, the same talents, and the same abilities, but we all were created to be different in our own unique way. Have you ever noticed twins? Some are identical, but when you get to know them, you will find out their differences. We can look at it just like that. Some of us have many things in common, some of us work great as a team, some of us share the same views, but when you get to know a person on an individual level, you will find out that we are not identical because we all have different spirits and personalities which makes us custom-made. It's up to us to choose God as our CEO, look at ourselves as being our own boss because we have a free will of choices. Those that we surround ourselves with are our coworkers. God is the one that created us. He wants to be our CEO. How does it look for us to tell the person who created the business how we are going to run the business without consulting with the headfirst? If you are going to launch Love as your Career, we must follow our CEO first. Not to mention he is the one that hires us for the job. I'm not saying we will always agree with his way. I'm not saying that we would never feel like we are being treated fairly. I'm not saying we will always see things from his perspective. I'm not saying there won't be times when you feel like giving up and want to quit. I know it may be a time when we will feel like he doesn't have our back. During times of not understanding what our CEO is doing, we must keep our eyes on the big picture of our destiny and focus on where we want our purpose to lead us. Not knowing the direction your life is headed ultimately turns into regrets and disappointments. Allow your CEO to be your guide. Psalm 119:105 says: "Thy word is a lamp unto my feet and a light unto my path." By reading God's words and standing firm on his promises, he will guide us into a fruitful life that will result in making the right choices. His words also state in Matthew 6:33 "that if we seek him first and his righteousness, all other things will be added unto us.

When we stop trying to follow the worldly life's standards, we can then come in agreement with the Heavenly Father by living under the CEO's wisdom and knowledge. We can launch a life of possibilities and opportunities of growing into Love. Without Love and forgiveness, there is no hope. Without hope, there is no progress. It's a domino effect. God loved us first because he created us. By God loving us, we can love ourselves. Why because we are special, we were uniquely made; we are just right and more than enough for God. We are made from his image. The reason some of us may not comprehend being in his likeness is because we don't see as God sees. We don't think as God thinks. Sometimes what he does and why he does it is a mystery. This may be why sometimes we call ourselves getting mad with God for disappointments in our lives. A lot of times, we are looking at what other people see, we are talking the way other people talk, and we are thinking the other way people are thinking. We are even acting the way others are acting. To the point that we get confused and don't know where we are in our own lives. Allow your CEO, the (Heavenly Father) to guide you so that with discipline and our efforts to have a willing mind and heart, we can proactively make a positive impact on our coworkers. We can help those around us and those that we encounter to launch love into a meaningful career that brings benefits to everyone individually.

God has many benefits that he is willing to offer when we are seeking opportunity. He offers his son Jesus, the Holy Spirit, and unconditional Love. Your benefits include the characteristics of having a spirit of Discernment, Patience, Kindness, Humbleness, Joy, Peace, and Generosity.

It's a good thing about having our Heavenly Father as our CEO because he has many positions available. He requires that we all be willing to lead but on different levels. Out of all my years of living, it was only a few years back that I realized that living for God, no matter what position I've been placed in. My position is important! It's not what the world says that makes it important; it's the position that I have been led into from my CEO, the (Heavenly Father) that hired me that makes it important. God doesn't look at your salary to determine how important your position is. When he puts you on your assignment and gives you a project to do, he wants you to fulfill it to the best of your ability. He will make certain that we are compensated for our labor to him. God wants to say to us in Matthew 25:21, "Well done good and faithful servant, you have been faithful of a few things. Therefore, I will put you in charge of many things."

If you look at this verse, God did not give a title to anyone. He addressed everyone as servants. If you have ever questioned why you were put on this earth? Which I'm certain is a common question. It tells you right here in this scripture that we are servants. Everyone was created by God. Therefore, we are here on earth to be servants! Servants for All Mighty God. We are to serve for a cause and a purpose to others and not just ourselves. I hope that this is not disappointing to you. However, if you are not serving on this earth for the upbuilding of God's kingdom and with the right motives, guess what! You are not serving your purpose, and you are not launching Love as your Career.

One of the most rewarding accomplishments of launching Love as our Career is when we empower others. This will take Love, Forgiveness, Patience, Motivation, Inspiration, Leadership, Passion, Commitment, Service, and Communication, which will be beneficial in your spiritual 401-investment plan. You are ultimately making an investment within yourself. These are developed qualities that don't require money but are necessary for us to offer our efforts of serving others and being faithful to God.

The last thing I want to talk about in this chapter is maintaining a peaceful relationship with ourselves and others. Why, because relationship matters. We should work on becoming experienced peacemakers in our own lives in order to influence peace into other people's lives. Matthew 5:9 "says blessed are the peacemakers for they shall be called the children of God." Romans 12:18 says, "If at all possible, as much it depends on you, live peaceable with all men." If we find ourselves not being able to get along with certain individuals, or maybe they don't get along with us, we can still initiate peace in our own lives. Once we learn how to get along with ourselves, we can then learn how to get along with others. We should not be so eager to escape our challenges with others. We are sometimes hurt by those who we love the most. We feel a sense of betrayal, but we should practice reconciling our differences. Jesus was betrayed by one of his disciples. Matthew 26: 14-16. Before Jesus also left the earth, he had also forgiven those who tortured him, mocked him, and blasphemed him. Our Heavenly Father's hands will not touch spirits that do not release forgiveness. When you release forgiveness, you release the power of the Holy Spirit that lives within us after we are saved. Jesus knew what it felt like to have the enemy disapprove of us. If your Love has been broken, it can be healed, it can be rebuilt, and it can be restored. I didn't say it would be easy, but this is required of us. There may be times that we may feel that others don't deserve our forgiveness, or the relationship should not be reconciled. It takes time for some relationships to be recreated. That's when we can still love from a distance because some relationships are toxic. Some relationships are worth saving and some are not, but we can still love others in the process because God is Love, and there is no other way for eternal life with him. We must keep in mind that we should be asking for forgiveness every day by God's grace. Romans 12:21 says, "Do not overcome evil with evil but overcome evil with good." Thinking of ways to get revenge and acting on it is not our place. It's not our responsibility to take matters into our own hands. Romans 12: 19 Our Heavenly Father says, "Vengeance is his and that he will repay." When you mean someone evil, it can change your life in a very negative way. The moment that we get caught off guard and lose our temper, we can lose what is meaningful. Our job, our life, we could go to prison or jail, and just as worse, it can shut down our blessings. We should eliminate bitterness, strife, hate, and jealousy against anyone by launching Love As our Career. Another powerful enemy that we face is not just our actions but our tongue. Proverbs 18:21. Proverbs 15:1 says, "A soft answer turns away wrath, harsh words stir up anger. Love no matter what has happened in the past. Love no matter what is happening in the present. The first greatest commandment Jesus said was to love the Lord with all your heart, soul, and mind. The Lord's second commandment is to love your neighbor as yourself. Matthew 22:37-39. I truly believe that once we launch Love as our Career by producing Love, building Love, showing Love, expressing Love, and giving Love. We don't have to look for Love in all the wrong places because Love will always find us.

CHAPTER 12 – SPIRITUAL CAREER INVESTMENT HANDBOOK

*Showing kindness through our actions is a selfless quality to have towards others, whether they deserve it or not. We don't have to manipulate others to get what we want or base our kindness on how others treat us.

*Staying focused on what is important to our Heavenly Father.

*Refrain from influences by those that are not following our Heavenly Father's ways.

*We as believers should Love the sinner but hate the sin.

*We are commanded by Jesus Christ to love our enemies and forgive our persecutors.

*Our words should always build up one another, comfort and encourage others.

*A believer has a responsibility to give a personal testimony as a way of expressing what our creator has already done and is doing in oneself life.

*Believers have the authority through Jesus Christ to claim His promises through scriptures that apply to any situation.

*Investing in souls being saved is a pursuit to gain eternal value.

*Living by our Heavenly Father's principles will equip us to make decisions in any circumstances that we may encounter.

*Studying our Heavenly Father's words is the only way for us as believers to recognize his will for our life.

*Praying daily to the Heavenly Father will make us sensitive to his ways.

*Teach our children how to tune into hearing from our Heavenly Father instead of listening to evil influences.

*Trusting and Obeying in our Father's will, gives us courage, and strengthens our faith while glorifying him in the process.

*Accepting Jesus Christ as your personal savior, we are guaranteed eternal life.

*Raising our children with a biblical foundation is one of the greatest gifts to give them.

*As followers of Jesus Christ, we must devote ourselves into leading people to meet Jesus by demonstrating Love.

*It is our personal responsibility to reach the lost in an imperfect world.

*We may be working hard for our own goals, but if it's not for our creator's purpose, it's just a wasted effort.

*It is our primary responsibility as parents to invest our time, maintain patience, give instructions and show Love which is necessary to develop our children.

*As our Love grows for our Heavenly Father, so also should we grow hatred for evil

*Salvation is not just an experience to be enjoyed; it's a gift to be shared.

*Surrender to the Holy Spirit to empower and guide us through our character, conversation, and conduct.

*Since the earth is not our permanent home, we must be mindful not to become attached to the things it offers that aren't eternal.

*Worship and Praise is about honoring and reverencing our Heavenly Father with our mind, heart, and spirit.

*Invest in our Heavenly Father's kingdom the first 10% of our fruit through obedience and trusting Him to provide for our needs.

*In order to stay on our Heavenly Father's life journey, we must allow his scriptures to guide us into making corrections in our behavior through our heart, mind, and spirit

*Make a habit of praying for others.

*If we utilize our faith, our Heavenly Father will always take full responsibility for the consequences of our obedience.

*Teach our children the right way to handle money, earn honestly, give generously, save intelligently and learn strong work values.

*Instruct our children on how to operate under the authority of parents, schools, church leaders, and our government.

*It will be wise to stay focused on our Heavenly Father's instructions and trust the Holy Spirit with our consciousness.

*When we humbly serve others, we can expect to experience a fullness of joy and satisfying life.

*Our life career goals should be established with a foundation of living Godly through reliance on the Holy Spirit.

*We as believers must set the standards of serving God faithfully and following his will rather than our own.

*Every task that our Heavenly Father asks us to do, whether big or small, is important to the kingdom of God. It's not the task that he looks at but our attitude in acting out the task.

*Prayer is not for the purpose of our Heavenly Father to follow our plan, but it's for us to ask for his plan.

*If we allow ourselves to get comfortable in the security of earth success, we will overlook life from an eternal perspective.

*Retire from pride and arrogance because it will deviate a person from our Heavenly Father's path of life.

*Trust in our Heavenly Father's unconditional Love rather than people's conditional Love.

*Prayer is not self-centered around a list of requests; it is having conversations with our Heavenly Father that builds a relationship with him as we put our faith in him that he knows best.

*When we are on an assignment, whether it's working on a job or owning a business, we have the opportunity to serve and show Love towards others.

*Eliminate your hunger for something or someone to fill your emptiness and acknowledge that only our Heavenly Father can satisfy your appetite.

*As a believer, we are obligated to exhibit Jesus Christ through our behavior and conversations.

*When facing a difficult situation, our Heavenly Father requires us to wait on him through faith, humility, patience, and courage. Relying on him and his timing is one of the most important choices to make during the process.

*When we rely more on earthly riches more than we do our Heavenly Father, it becomes a sin.

*Praying in the name of Jesus settles the agreement that secured your request to God's will.

*Align your thoughts, attitude, and beliefs with biblical teachings.

*Create a balanced schedule in order to maintain a healthy relationship with family, friends, and others.

*Consistently spend private time with our Heavenly Father in order to obtain an intimate relationship with him and gain clear guidance.

*Do not allow work to consume you. Allow an adequate amount of exercise, recreation, and rest for enjoyment.

*Allow time at church and fellowship with other believers for worship.

*When we pursue the work of following Jesus Christ, we discover peace and blessings in the process.

*Fasting is a spiritual discipline commitment that is recommended to help us to center our attention towards the Heavenly Father and discover his will for our lives.

*Fasting and Praying are powerful practices we should acquire if we want to hear instructions from our creator.

*Our Father is pleased when we seek an opportunity to share our knowledge about Jesus with those that don't know him.

*Terminate anger quickly because it can turn into resentment, which can poison our thinking and behavior.

*If we permit someone we trust to give us an assessment of ourselves we can better position ourselves to make improvements.

*We should take the necessary steps and make the decision to accept salvation on earth because when we die, there will be no other opportunities.

*It's impossible to obtain a relationship with the Heavenly Father and His son Jesus Christ without spending time reading, studying, and the meditation his words.

*When we make the decision to surrender to our Heavenly Father and obey him in the process. We may have to suffer sometimes, so be prepared to make painful sacrifices, but our Heavenly Father will make certain that we are rewarded at the end.

*We should commit to becoming a valuable servant to God by placing our trust and obedience in him.

*We should view life's situation as a design to develop our faith, practice obedience, and gain spiritual maturity, and trusting God in the process.

*Our genuine need for Love comes from having a secure and intimate relationship with our Heavenly Father.

*Obedience to God's instructions leads us to greater opportunities and abundant blessings.

*When we obey our Heavenly Father's irrational plans, we are to listen carefully to the task for it to be carried out correctly and safely.

*Utilizing our faith with our Heavenly Father's promises will equip us with everything we need to do the work our creator has chosen for us.

*When the work of service is done in humble submission to the Holy Spirit, it produces a lasting value to our Father's purpose in us.

*Our responsibility as believers is to make time for those that are suffering and in need, even when it's inconvenient and uncomfortable.

Building a close relationship with our Heavenly Father will allow us to see ourselves, others, and our circumstances from his viewpoint.

*If we are willing to walk wisely and allow wisdom to take root in our spirit, our Father has promised to guide and protect us.

*When we comply with our creator's virtue desires, it will prevent us from entering foolish and sinful relationships that pull us away from God.

*Our trust in our Heavenly Father is produced when we think of past situations that our Father has provided us with, protected, and seen us through.

*We are saved by accepting Jesus Christ by faith and not by our good behavior and good deeds.

Consistent repentance and confession of sins is the pathway to a healthy relationship with Jesus Christ.

*As faithful servants, it is our responsibility to utilize our time, our ability, and finances to build God's kingdom.

*As God's children, we can keep his eternal benefits when we are saved, but when we are disobedient, we stand the chance of missing out on his best rewards.

*Seeking God is a lifelong commitment that requires consistency and perseverance.

*One of the most important pursuits in a believer's life, is building a relationship with our Heavenly Father.

12.1 - MAKING AN INVESTMENT FOR YOUR ETERNAL GOAL

Being Christ-Like requires more than just going to church, fellowshipping with believers, distributing church duties, and giving our tithes and offering. This is what we would do on days of having service. It requires a commitment of going out into the world and not just speaking of God but exhibiting who Jesus is through our work of service, compassion, sharing, caring, assisting, and encouraging others. It requires us to get out of our comfort zone. It's necessary to interrupt our schedules by putting someone else before us. It takes being inconvenient by investing in the lives of others and meeting their needs and loving others that are different than who we are. All believers are not called to be ministers, evangelists, priests, or bishops. However, we all are created to be disciples of our Heavenly Father by demonstrating his Love towards everyone.

Pride, unforgiveness, hatred, and lack of Love do not fit into our Father's handbook of life. Through our Heavenly Father's blessings of gifts and talents that lives within us, it's up to us to use these skills to please God almighty rather than just having them to please ourselves.

12.2 - COUNT YOUR BLESSINGS

It's less beneficial to have a relationship with the Heavenly Father when we go through life depending on ourselves. This leads to pride and arrogance. It's through our brokenness and helplessness that we can truly get to know our Heavenly Father and how important it is to have him in our lives. There was so much going on in the year "2020". A year that will never be forgotten. A year that I'm certain will go down in history. The virus of COVID-19, the elections, the protests of *Black Lives Matter*, suicide rates going up, Businesses being shut down, causing the highest rate imaginable for unemployment. People suffering with health challenges and even death not just relating to the virus. Overwhelming tragedies and no social gatherings even at our churches.

The one thing for certain that believers had in common was to trust our Heavenly Father. Without our dependence on God. Believing in his promises, trusting in his Love for us, through his grace and mercy, where would we be mentally, spiritually, emotionally, and relationally? I truly believe that if it wasn't for the prayers of the believers and the righteous, things would have been worst. Honestly, through all the chaos and the despair, we were still blessed in the process. Some of us were blessed more than imaginable.

12.3 - GRATITUDE THROUGH YOUR ATTITUDE

In a painful situation, expressing gratitude can be difficult. The apostle Paul in the bible knew his riches in Jesus Christ outweighed the earthly discomfort that he encountered. Paul knew that God had a plan for his life. Through our design gifts and spiritual empowerment, our Father promises to meet our every need with his resources and to provide us with his richest blessings. There are times that we define blessings as being rich with money and how much we possess. The scripture in proverbs mentions overworking to become rich. It is well received to have nice things and have an enormous bank account, but will it provide you with peace and satisfaction knowing that you are earthly rich and spiritually poor? Our Father will flourish us with his blessings because he is good, and his Love is everlasting. What spiritual believers must comprehend is that humans value being rich in their pockets, but Christ values being rich through our hearts. Ephesians 1:3.

12.4 - REACHING OUR GOALS THROUGH STRENGTH AND COURAGEOUSNESS

Most of the time, we are consumed with reaching our own personal goals. However, when we make the efforts to pursue what we want to accomplish, we don't always, if not at all, talk it over with our Heavenly Father for guidance. We then get disappointed when our plans don't work out or don't progress fast enough. Our success will be determined by our dependence on God. Our Father gives us the skills and talents and He give us the strength to fulfill our divine assignments. If we take the time to read some of the stories that took place in the Bible, we will see that many assignments were given by God. There are demonstration of historical people whose accomplishments were successful through their passion, motivation, and confidence in the Lord. One of God's promises was to be "strong and courageous, for I am with you." Joshua 1:9.

Having an action plan in place is one of the ways to help become successful. A calendar and a journal are the tools that can be used to help you get started with your goals. It's one thing to speak our goals into existence and it's another thing to have them written down and consistently looking over them to remind ourselves where we are going. Constantly being reminded will allow us to keep our eyes focused on our Heavenly Father's words and strive for the assignments that have been prepared for us to accomplish without deviating from it. There may be times when our Heavenly Father will lay upon our hearts to do something that we may feel inadequate to do. We may get caught up in fear of failure and the negative opinions of others. That is why it is good to know our Heavenly Father's words and what he has to say about us and believe that he is the one that will equip us to succeed.

Success is not measured based on whether we are able to draw a crowd or how much money we are bringing in, or the material things we can show off. That's what the world likes to have us believe. Success comes from our Heavenly Father's viewpoint. We are to trust the Holy Spirit by asking for our calling to be revealed. Whether our tasks are behind the scenes or in public, we are to give our best to the Lord. When we are under our Heavenly Father's authority, he will provide us with the skills and the promotions to achieve his plan. Our Father wants to use our life to further his kingdom, and in the process, he receives glorification. You may have made a name for yourself on earth, but will it be worth it if your name will never be known in heaven? We should never feel that someone's assignment is more important or greater than what we are doing. This is when we start feeling defeated and discouraged. If we focus on how to glorify God in the process of our success, we can be thankful and humble ourselves to give God credit for our success and be proud of what he is accomplishing through us. God's will is not for us to have impure motives and worthless tasks when we are motivated to succeed. Our success should be based on loving others enough so that our influence on others will not go in vain, but unbelievers will begin to desire the same passion, motivation, and Love for God while carrying out God's mission of becoming Christ-like.

Our Heavenly Father specializes in using people who aren't naturally qualified. On the earth, we may earn degrees to further learn a profession and make more money. Our Father gives us the mental strength to gain the knowledge and the courage to gain the skills. Have you ever wondered why two different people may go out for the exact same career but may not be as successful as the other person? We should not compare ourselves to others because it limits our accomplishments on our own personal level. God is not looking for showboats, undisciplined and proud people to deliver his plan. He searches for applicants that are humble, submissive, willing to obey, resilient, work as a team, and pursue love. Our Father looks at our resume for people with ordinary skills. Even if he sees that our strength has been weakened, he is more than capable of providing that. He is looking for those that have weaknesses. The CEO of our life is interviewing for positions that will be willing to allow themselves to be demonstrated through the Divine power of the Holy Spirit. The one that has created us is looking for candidates that will delight themselves in him so that our dependence can be displayed for his platform. If you have a resume that displays a lack of abilities, talents, and skills, our leader the Heavenly Father will support our inadequacies for his purpose if we are willing to be lead under his leadership.

A few examples of how our Heavenly Father used ordinary people in the Bible to succeed with the lack of human skills. Moses liberated a nation when only being an 80-year-old Shepard who was verbally impaired. The youngest son David was a Shepard who killed a giant with a small stone and later became Israel's king and a man after God's own heart. Paul became a great Christian leader. Years later, Paul became imprisoned and served jailed time. During this time in his life, he was experiencing adversity. Something great came out of his hardship. Paul had the courage to speak and minister to those he encountered, with the assisting of the Holy Spirit providing him with physical and mental stamina. Paul had become an effective servant by allowing the Holy Spirit to release its power through him for the purpose of our Father's will to be fulfilled. The apostle Paul relied upon the strength of the Father by staying faithful and never giving up. 2 Corinthians 12:9 says, "My grace is sufficient for you, for My strength is made perfect in weakness." Jesus Christ (son of God)

"His Name Is Faithful"

Our Father knows that sometimes we will face trials. When we do reach the mark of discouragement, our human nature will become weak, weary, tired, hopeless, and sometimes fearful, but God's words ask us to rely on his strength and courage and not our own. We may feel as if we have been pushed beyond our ability to endure. We may have been placed into a position of loneliness. The great awesome news is that when we belong to Jesus Christ, we can be assured that our Heavenly Father is always with us.

Our courage becomes more effective when we allow God's purpose to take effect in our life. Courage starts to develop in us when we recognize God's presence. A bitter-sweet testimony I would like to share about my sister Laverne whose faith was tested when she had been diagnosed with breast cancer. Laverne had gone to the doctor for her regular mammogram. At this doctor's visit, the doctors found a cyst on her breast. The doctors proceeded with attempting to try draining the cyst, but they became curious when they couldn't drain it. After realizing that it was a hard substance, they decided to do a biopsy. Laverne was nervous, but the doctor said everything would be okay. Being optimistic and a woman of faith, Laverne told herself that everything was alright and okay and that it was nothing. Two weeks had gone by before the results had come in, and then that's when her doctor had asked her to come into the office. While Laverne was in the waiting room, she had prayed to God that she would get a good report and that everything would be alright. Other patients were in the waiting room as well, giving their stories and their testimonies of being cancer survivors. Laverne was praying with them and telling them that everything was good. Just before going back to be seen by her doctor, a few patients gave her their best wishes. She thanked them and went back to another room, not knowing that the news was, in fact, that Laverne had breast cancer in her right breast. The doctor explained that there were two lumps found. One measured around 3 centimeters, which the second one was a little smaller than the first one. It was explained that the lumps really didn't have a stage to them, but it was more likely that she would need to start treatment. When they told her the news, she was like, "No, that can't be...No... It can't be. "Everything went blank," she said. She felt like she couldn't hear anything. She felt like she couldn't breathe. She was just stunned by the news. Laverne had spoken to herself, saying, "I eat right, I exercise, I pray, I pray for others who have cancer. I don't eat all that crazy food." All this stuff ... "me... I have cancer?" She broke down crying. Everything just went black. Her doctor asked, "Who could they call for her?" she said, "Nobody." Her words were, "I don't want to live." "I want to die." "I don't want anything." "I don't want anything." "Just let me die." Laverne became very emotional to the point of falling down crying in disbelief. She remembered the doctor telling her that "everything would be alright, Mrs. Mays." Laverne recalls her doctor repeating, "everything is going to be alright, Mrs. Mays, and "It's alright." The doctor said, "You got your family, and you got your children." "You can't let this beat you." "You're going to be good," her doctor added. Laverne replied, "No, I don't want it." Laverne said. Laverne's doctor eventually called her husband and told him what was going on. When her husband heard the news, she could tell that his heart dropped just because he had been in this situation before with a family member, and the situation did not turn out well. Laverne called one of our oldest sisters and told her the prognosis. Even though our sister was talking to Laverne, Laverne was not trying to hear anything because she was in disbelief at what was happening. Through all the chaos, Laverne never questioned God. She never asked God why? Once Laverne got herself together. Our sister prayed with Laverne, and Laverne's husband had questions of his own. After leaving the doctor's office, Laverne cried in the car, cried at home, and all through the night. She just couldn't sleep. Laverne received the news on a Thursday the day before her birthday. The very next day, going to work on her birthday Laverne said, "a peace had come over he." She felt no worry, but she still felt like she was in a dream. Finally, the shock was over. Her next concern was how she was going to tell her daughters. She was really scared and hesitant about telling them without them worrying about her. Just the thought of affecting her daughters negatively was enabling her to concentrate and function well, which would lead to being mentally depressed. "How was she going to tell her daughters that she has breast cancer?" Laverne's concern was the fact that her younger daughter's mother had passed from breast cancer just a few weeks before. Adding to that, her oldest two daughters have friend's moms who had cancer or some form of illness. She was contemplating telling them and just keeping it to herself. She was saying to herself, "should she just keep things to herself and whatever happens, just let it happen? They wouldn't know," she thought selfishly to herself. However, knowing who she was putting her trust in, Laverne put her faith to work by asking God how she should tell her daughters the news and how she could go about it without affecting their lives in a negative way. Soon after, Laverne decided to tell her daughters. She knew she had to do it. She called them together to meet with her. She gave them the news, and that discussed it. Thank God they handled it better than she expected. As a matter of fact, they were the ones that ended up encouraging her. God had already predestined things to fall into place. Laverne went back to the doctors after having many appointments, tests, MRI's ,blood work, and CAT scans. Amazingly all the results came back wonderful. No side effects or anything. The doctors kept saying that she needed chemo and radiation, but she said, "No." Laverne was very stern about not having any of those treatments. The doctors communicated that without the treatments, it was possible for cancer to spread in other areas of her body. Right then, she said, "Not again," and confirmed that she was already healed. She replied, "When God healed me, it was a done deal." Even though the doctors tried to persuade her and compromise what she had believed, Laverne stood firm on her decision not to take the treatments. She claimed and stood on the promises of God. She began to pray from sunup to sundown. She went to sleep praying. She woke up praying. She listened to all her praise and worship music throughout the day. She refrained from television. Laverne was on a Jesus high, remaining in God's presence. She meditated on all the healing scriptures. She placed her hands on her breast and just talked to God all day and all night. She also went on to pray for others who had cancer. She just kept the joy that was inside her. The beautiful thing is that she didn't hold anything against God. She didn't hold anything against people. She just kept her laughter, her joy, and her sense of humor. She still had fun with her family. She continued going places and living her life. You wouldn't have even known that anything was wrong with her because she didn't allow her situation to change her. A few weeks passed; the doctors went along with her decision of not moving forward with the treatments. However, they did say that she had to have a surgery called mastectomy. She had peace about the surgery, she was without doubt, and she still trusts God that she has been healed. During the weeks of another round of testing, her lymph node was good, and there was no cancer in her body anywhere. "God is able," she says, "and he can do it!" What turned out to be a nightmare and seems to have been a tragedy turned into a testimony of making a new, improved Laverne? Laverne now feels on top of the world. Laverne told herself that in the year 2021, she would give herself the title "A New Beginning." Like Job in the Bible, when you go through a storm, bad news, or a life-changing situation such as she did. It does us good to search stories in the Bible that relate to your situation. Job had a story in the Bible where he went through with having boils, sickness, and health disparities. God allowed Job to experience those things for a reason. Job went through all these things without cursing God even though his wife told him to. Instead, Job prayed, fasted, and stayed aligned with God's words and his promises. God totally healed Job and gave Job back so much more extra. Job dropped his robe and said, "naked I came into the world, naked will I go." Laverne didn't go naked, but she did cut her hair. She felt fabulous and beautiful inside and out. She's at the point where she wants to tell everyone. She feels that God has now given her this anointing on her life for her to tell people how good God is. Now when she prays, she knows that it is already done within the will of God. She sees the results of God's promises. Now when she sees others that say they have cancer, this warm feeling of compassion comes over her. They inspire her to tell them also to just trust God and watch him work. Others will call her and say, "Laverne, you are an Angel because what you said is the truth." Laverne thankful to God for her family, pastor, and all her friends and loved ones who prayed for her day in and day out.

CHAPTER 13 – GOD GOT IT

I would like to share a personal story with you. This story is about my youngest son Xavier. Xavier was diagnosed with asthma at an early age. It never really stopped him from participating in activities, but he would get hit hard with an attack when certain times of the season would change. It had gotten to the point where he would never have perfect attendance in school. I was almost certain every year that it was one award he wasn't going to get. "Perfect Attendance Award." Even when he would play sports, he couldn't reach his highest potential because he would become short-winded, and it would take some of his energy away. Especially when playing basketball. I continued as a mother to pray for his healing. I learned over time that when an uncomfortable situation isn't left up to me, I must just pray. That brings me to the prayer, "God grant me the serenity to accept the things I cannot change, the courage to change the things I can, and the wisdom to know the difference." I do have to say that along with this journey, I discovered that with this asthma swimming, and other activities could help strengthen the lungs and can become very effective with getting better over time. Also, just a little talk with Jesus can have a great impact on this sickness. I don't want to excuse the fact that every child is different, but it's worth looking into certain activities, especially if it is approved by their doctors. To keep the story going, praise God! Xavier has not had any asthma episodes after 12 years old. Thank the Lord, Glory to his mighty name! That was the history of the story, and now I will continue the story of God's goodness towards Xavier. Throughout high school, Xavier couldn't figure out exactly what he wanted to do when he graduated. He was accepted at a theme high school as a junior ROTC cadet. We were very excited about it because, as parents, we wanted to see him in a great school that really challenges student's abilities. It was not easy, but as a parent, I stayed involved. I built relationships with the teachers, and I encouraged Xavier to do more than what was expected of him. 12th-grade year, Xavier entered a barbering class to learn a trade. When you have a close relationship with your children, the better off you will be as a parent because you can pick up things just by being around them. I pretty much knew this wasn't Xavier's passion, and I think he knew it too. Often our kids make quick decisions because they don't have a clear direction. Doesn't that sound familiar with what we do as adults? I prayed, and I asked Xavier to pray as we too prayed together that our Heavenly Father would give Xavier clear assurance path he should take for his future. Speaking of which, it's a good idea to teach our children how to pray because we are not going to always be there. They must learn how to pray not only for others but for themselves. I recognized during that journey with Xavier not to focus on the destination but be in tune with the moment before us. In the beginning, I started to feel a little anxiety because I was like, Lord, "I feel like I did everything I could to get my son through this challenging school and just for him not to have any direction, just don't seem like your character." But God.... shortly after Xavier graduated, he was like, "mom, I want to go to the military." Tears came to my eyes just writing this story. "I asked, are you sure?" He said, "yes, mom, I'm sure."

114

Let me just say that this was the young man that wanted to take a break in his senior year from ROTC because he just wanted a break from being in the program for three consecutive years, which I didn't agree with the decision, but I did approve his decision. Back to the story, as soon as I heard a "yes mom!" from him, Xavier's voice sounded so assured, so strong, confident, and affirmed. I knew it had to be the Lord because, surprisingly, I had no hesitation in my reaction. I wasn't worried, and I wasn't scared. I felt very confident in the Lord. I knew then that this would be the direction Xavier would begin. After that confirmation, do you think that it's the end of the story? Nope! When Xavier went to get his physical for the United States Army, they first stated that he was underweight and had to gain a certain number of pounds. The recruiter also called to let us know that the doctor that had examined Xavier discovered that he had scoliosis, which is a medical condition that caused the spine to curve and could get worse over time. If the curve gets too bad, it can cause problems to the back, which would interfere with his job as a military soldier. After this, I continued to pray to God.

The purpose of our prayers to our Father is not to get him to work it out the way we want it, but to work it out his way and in His timing because he knows what's best for us. Even though Xavier wanted this, and I wanted this for him, I prefer it to be approved by God Almighty. It was better for him to be protected under God than trusting the unknown and the unexpected. A few months passed, even though this was still the same year of graduating from high school. Things were finally coming together. The recruiter called and said that Xavier's orthopedic doctor approved Xavier for going into the military. During the waiting period, Xavier continued to eat more which caused him to pick up more weight. Guess what, though?

Xavier still had another hiccup. Once Xavier entered the military, he called me, stating that he may not be able to stay in the military. My mouth dropped, and my spirit became very low. The reason he said so was that he had to do some training. He had passed all areas in his physical training except for his running. This was his second try, and if he didn't meet the timely standard on the third try, he would have been discharged. Let me remind you that earlier in the story I told you that Xavier suffered from asthma in his early years up until about 12 years old. That was the one thing that always stopped him. When he overexerts himself, his breathing shortens, which makes it challenging for him to push himself. As soon as we got off the phone, I broke into tears. The most amazing thing was not giving up on God. I still trusted him even though I didn't see what was ahead. That is why it is so good to know our father's character, have a relationship with him, and learn his promises. When things go wrong and not the way you expect, even with great disappointment, the Holy Spirit will bring back in remembrance of scriptures you have studied and meditated on. The Holy Spirit will also remind us of how faithful God has been in the past. God is fully capable and willing to continue being faithful. I went outside and started walking and listening to my praise and worship music in my neighborhood. It's like once I got in tune with the words of the song, I felt so confident in the Lord. I thought about the scripture that God says, "He knows the plan he has for us, to give us hope for our future" Jeremiah 29:11. I also remembered the story about David starting out being just a young Shephard boy. David had a physique of being small and had very little strength. However, as David got older, God had appointed David as a king. God didn't focus on how small David's statue was, and He admired how David's heart was towards him. I know Xavier has a genuine heart. Not just for his family but also for other people. I know that God was looking at Xavier's heart and what he could do for our country that someone else wouldn't want to do. During the decision-making process, Xavier was willing to step out of his comfort zone, step into faith, and show courageousness and strength. I would say about two days later, Xavier called and stated that he was getting ready to perform his last physical run. I said, "son, before you step out on that track, say to yourself that I can do all things through Christ Jesus, who strengthens me!" A couple of days later, Xavier called and told me the awesome news! He had passed his running test! Xavier has now been in the United States Army for almost four years and has not once looked back. I'm not certain if he will make it a career, but I'm confident that God will continue to order his steps.

Lesson to be learned: Don't give up on God because he won't give up on us!

13.1 - THE REWARD OF WAITING ON GOD THROUGH OBEDIENCE

When we feel a need to move ahead on something we want to accomplish, waiting on our Heavenly Father can be a difficult discipline to obtain. Waiting on the Lord is essential to living a successful, rewarding Christian life. Through our obedience, reaping our Father's blessings will follow a great purpose for his plans for us. It will be a mistake to be overly eager and act on our own without getting clear directions when the time is right. We can miss out on our Father's best when we step ahead of the game without the instructions of our CEO (our creator). Without prayer of asking for guidance and direction and going through the waiting process, we can miss out on the blueprints that our father is preparing for us and the promotion we will receive. One of the essential requirements for obedience is trusting God. Proverbs 3:5.

Our obedience results from our foundation of having faith. We must believe that our Holy God is who he says that he is. We must trust in his plans, his timing, and his method for our life. As part of our daily lives, we must wait with an attitude of trust until we are certain of what God wants us to do. If we get impatient, we often rely on our own understanding hoping that our Father will approve and give us his blessing for our own self decisions. During the waiting period, obedience is required when we don't totally understand what's going on and when things are unclear. However, Our Father makes himself responsible for the consequences in our obedience to him. Our waiting upon the Lord is time for preparation. Holy God has us waiting while he coordinates situations to line up with his will. Sometimes the Lord has work to accomplish in us before we are ready to handle what he has planned for our future. Waiting helps to strengthen us spiritually. Waiting patiently strengthens our faith by trusting in Holy God with confidence that in time, we will know what to do. Our Father has promised to give us supernatural peace when we wait on him. We get caught up in our daily responsibilities, our multitasking, and juggled life that we end up emotionally and physically tired. We are at the point of exhaustion, even for the Lord. Take time to focus on Holy God. Align our pace with his steps and take the time to rest and receive the empowerment of the Holy Spirit that our Father generously gives to us so that we can wait on him through obedience and the great reward that follows. Read these three instructions carefully as suggestions to help you through the process of waiting in obedience.

Pray: Having a relationship with the Father

Meditate: Pursue wisdom through scriptures

Listen: Spending quiet time with the Lord allows the Holy Spirit to give us a clear mind to be in tune with our Father's directions by bringing to our remembrance through the scriptures what we have learned and how it will apply to our situation.

13.2 - RECOGNIZING OUR WORTH IN SOCIETY

When we ignore or turn away from the responsibility of what is best needed for our nation, country, community, and neighborhoods, we suffer the consequences. We get to the point of not working as a team. When we consider ourselves to be more advance than others, we start to become self-led leaders. We then find our environment and society to be in chaos. Through all the division that we may experience or see in life, our behavior is caused by strife, pride, and greed. We deliberately fall short of God's standard of righteous living; God does not fire us from his employment and turns his back on us. Instead, God loves us unconditionally, and his grace will keep us employed even when we don't meet his expectations. Pride will cause us to derail from the perfect plan of God and prevent us from reaching the full potential that God wants to do in us and through us. Strife causes us to be rebellious against one another and it will lead us into discord and conflicts in our behavior. Greed will cause us to be selfish, ruthless, and out of touch with our society. The world may want us to envision the meaning of success by absorbing into our own self - dependent and self-righteousness, but that's when our arrogance starts to control our way of thinking and our actions. We may sometimes allow pride, strife, and greed to take root in our life, but we must recognize how the world has structured our worth in society. When we have not exhibited humbleness, compassion, and empathy towards our society. Adversity may be one of the adversaries that we go up against in order to start depending on God and not ourselves. Only then, when we reach for hope in Jesus Christ, we are no longer a slave to the world. The world may look at holiness and being submissive to our Heavenly Father offensive. Reverencing and honoring our Heavenly Father may bring on criticism instead of praise and approval. However, if we take a stand and live out our spiritual worth through the faith of our God, our Father, our Jehovah, our creator, our worth will not just be for external purposes, but he will give us internal worth that is made to last a lifetime.

a. Accountability Partner

It is recommended that everyone should have someone that can account for them. It's called a mentor or a confidant. Someone that can see when we are blinded by our situation or seeing from the outside with a different perspective. Someone that is strong when we are weak. Someone that offers counseling and encouragement. A spirit-filled believer who will offer Godly wisdom based on scriptures. Someone who accepts and loves us as we are but confronts us with enough courage when we are wrong. Someone who truly looks out for our best interest. It's very important that we are aware of who this person or persons in our life is so that the relationship can be bonded on trust, honesty, and love for one another. Let's pray and ask God for these types of relationships with someone and ask him to reveal the right persons to us if we don't have this individual or individuals in our life already.

b. Forgiveness in the Midst of Unforgiveness

Forgiveness can be defined as letting go past resentment and having the right mindset of not returning the hurt. This is God's way because he has asked us to forgive ourselves and those who don't seem to deserve our Forgiveness. Unforgiveness can be defined as getting justice by taking matters into our own hands or getting back at whatever or whoever that have hurt us. Hurt may take time to heal, but with a willing heart. God can help us to forgive ourselves and others from a deserved punishment that should have led to major consequences. Our Father wants us to release the hurt that was done unto us so that we can have peace within. He wants us to be willing to forgive as we would like to be forgiven. If we get all bent out of shape and don't follow the standard of God's forgiveness plan, there is no point of establishing an opportunity of a lifetime in God's kingdom. One of our most challenging tasks as believers is forgiving those who have seriously hurt us. There is a process of growth and maturity to be accomplished. There may be a confession to be made or communication with the other person on how hurt we are. We can also take the initiative to ask our father to examine us as well by asking if there is anything within us that needs to be removed and forgiven. We have the right and privilege to ask the Heavenly Father for the same grace and leaving the judgment to our creator. If we allow the typical agitation of unforgiveness to rule our performance, it will cause the development of rooted bitterness. Recalling old and painful memories can slip back into our mind, and into our heart, and stir up emotions of anger and the actions of injustice. Even when the hurt is deep, this will not be a reason to rationalize your doings to get back the hurt. Instead, pray for compassion towards others and thank God for his gift of enabling us the opportunity to learn how to forgive just as he has forgiven us. Allow yourself time to heal, but in the process of forgiveness, start showing humility, where our mind will be at peace, our heart will be filled with love, and our merits will be plenty.

13.3 - WHAT DOES OUR BENEFITS PACKAGE INCLUDE?

*Our Heavenly Father promises to guide and protect us if we walk wisely. (Proverbs 4:6). "Do not forsake wisdom, and she will protect you."

*Reading Biblical Principals will assist us with transformation thinking and help us to rightly respond to situations so that we can get through our challenges in order to live out God's purpose. (Romans 12:2). "Do not conform to the pattern of this world but be transformed by the renewing of your mind. Then you will be able to test and approve what is pleasing to God's perfect will."

*We can do all things through our Heavenly Father, who strengthens us. (Philippians 4:13)

*Even though we will go through challenges, our experiences in life are the key lessons to be learned for future testimonies, encouraging others, and having a growing loving relationship with others. (John 15:13) "Greater love hath no man than a man lay down his life for his friends."

*Our Father's grace does not give us permission to sin, but by asking for Forgiveness, he gives us the opportunity to continuously pursue righteousness. (John 1:9). If we confess our sins, he is faithful and just and will forgive us our sins and purify us from all unrighteousness."

*We have the promise and the assurance of God's promises to guide us into a loving career. (Psalm 32:8.) "I will instruct you and teach you in the way which you should go. I will counsel you with my eye upon you."

*Demonstrating the words of God in love to influence believers and unbelievers that will help those that are hurting and put us in the position of being a great leader. (Proverbs 11:14). "Where there is no guidance, peoples fall, but in an abundance of counselors, there is safety."

*We will have the opportunity to see Jesus Christ and our loved ones that have gone to glory when this earthly life is over. (Titus 2:13). Looking for that blessed hope and the glorious appearing of the great God and our savior Jesus Christ."

*Through prayer, faith, and hope, we can go to the Heavenly Father with all our concerns. (Psalms 55:22). Cast all your cares on the Lord, and he will sustain you he will never let the righteous be forsaken."

*We can rely on the Holy Spirit to equip us and strengthen us in our weaknesses. (John 14:26). "The Holy Spirit whom the Father will send in my name will teach you all things and remind you of everything I have said to you."

*Dedicating our time to know and experience God is an essential plan of taking steps to have a satisfying lifestyle. (John 17:3). "Now this is eternal life: that they know you, the only true God and Jesus Christ whom you have sent."

*When we pursue diligence by making time in our schedule for regular study and prayer, we can strive to know and understand God's ways. (2 Timothy 2:15). "Study to show thyself approve unto God. A worker who does not need to be ashamed and who correctly handles the word of truth."

*Walking in the obedience of our Father, we will live prosperously, and our days will be prolonged in the land that we will possess. Deut. 5:3. The lord made not this covenant with our ancestors, but with us who lives today."

13.4 - OPPOSITIONS GOING AGAINST YOUR POSITION

Oppositions go against something or someone. We will have oppositions going against us, but it's how we will handle them that makes the difference. In the year 2020, we faced politicians going against each other. The White House was an uproar. It came down to getting the White House to empathize with the American people's situation of going through unemployment, loved ones passing during the COVID-19 virus, and schools not being safe to return to normal because of high cases of the virus remaining. We saw Black Lives Matters issues, Police Brutality, Riots, more cases of homelessness, and hopelessness. Employees that were working but not feeling safe for their health because of working during a pandemic. Financial uncertainty for some. Small businesses not being able to stay open and even others that weren't able to continue to pay rent or mortgage.

Opposition is unavoidable if we are on this earth in this lifetime. I recall many times when I suffered opposition in the workplace. Even though I felt like I was putting out positive energy, there still were times I felt like I was going through the motion all by myself. It seemed that numbers were more important than customer service. A shortage of staff left employees overwhelmed with work. There were limitations on promotions. Leaders were not performing professionally nor were they trained properly. I felt like later in my career, after being in hospitality, the morale was slowly diminishing. I had opposition going against me by not being who my personality and professionalism allowed me to be. Which eventually demolished the point of my job remaining rewarding. The only thing I knew to do was keep my faith, pray to God and ask for direction. The lesson that I learned during the process is when we focus our attention on our Heavenly Father and get the attention off on what's going on around us. God will allow the opposition to reverse itself in your favor.

An awesome testimony of how God took my opposition that went against my position and turned it around for my good. (Romans 8:28). "We know that all things work together for the good of those who love God and are called according to his purpose. It was the year 2020 when I was first furloughed, and then on May 1, 2021, my job, who I worked for 23 years of service called me and stated that because of the COVID 19 virus, I had to be let go along with many others. I can't even say I was devastated because I was already getting burnt out in my position and felt like I was reaching a dead end. Not to mention my mom's health was decreasing, and I knew this would give me more time to spend time her without having to call out from my job. I know prior to this whole pandemic, I had fasted and prayed for two years, January of 2018 and 2019, for three weeks. No sugar, no starches & no meats. I wrote down exactly what I was fasting for. I know on the top of my list was finding a new direction in life. Not just a new direction but a career that would show me my purpose in life. In 2019 it was placed on my heart to pay as many bills as possible off that I could and start budgeting my money. I did just that. Sometimes we don't know the reason or even understand why we are doing something, but when that inner spirit asks you to do something, well, I just think you may need to follow it. Would you know? The pandemic hit the entire world, so when my job called and gave me the news, it was sad but a relief at the same time. This was when I trusted God the most. This is when you must know God enough to say this is not my will Lord but yours. I didn't have many bills because I was paying them off anyway. I also had the privilege of staying in my parents' home because I was their caregiver for some years until they are now both passed. I listened to a lot of motivational speakers. These were the summer months, so I went to early morning walks and listened to my inspirational songs on how God will take care of you. I love the song Deitrick Haddon "Have your Way", & "Resting Place", Donnie McClurkin, "I Need You," "Tye Tibbett," What can I do," Travis Green (Intentional) & (Made a Way), Tasha Cobb (Fill me up). The Holy Spirit then gave me the permission of wanting to write a book. If I would have kept working, it's very possible that I would have never thought to write a book. Even though at first, I didn't know what I wanted to write about. I prayed on it. I had one of the greatest experiences of trusting God when he sat me down during my opposition, and I didn't know what to do next but pray, focus and meditate on him. Now, my new position has been replaced over my opposition.

CHAPTER 14 – BUILD ON RESILIENCE

14.1 – BUILDING RESILIENCE BY RELYING ON OUR FAITH

Resilience is not a word that I heard a lot about growing up. Resilience was my faith in God. Resilience is a good example of how a rubber band works. It stretches with flexibility to quickly bounce back. We all have or will face struggles, challenges, difficulty, and uncomfortable situations during our life. This is when our faith + our resilience will have to step in and get us through. As I've worked around many young adults, I have discovered that many have not grasped the ability to exercise their mental stamina. It may not be their fault. Things have changed since I grew up and became an adult. Children are being raised differently. When I was raising my children, they had choices on certain things, but when it was time to make the choices for them, I did just that. We must start out young practicing mental strength. It's just like exercising. If you are not used to doing it, it hurts at first. As we continue consistently doing it, our bodies become better prepared to endure. I really would like to see more of our young adults strengthening their patience with their faith to become resilient. With all the uncertainty that we are facing today, it's time to not only exercise our physical body but our mental well being as well. This can be practice by enduring patience, adapting to life's circumstances and accepting things that can't be changed, and moving forward with what's in our control. This will not mean that there will be times that we won't hurt or be disappointed. This will mean that we can try seeing things from a different view with a positive and realistic mindset. This type of thinking will keep us moving forward instead of thinking backward. We are well built to expand our thinking and make changes where necessary. It's all part of growing. If we don't take the initiative to stretch ourselves, we don't know how far we can go. Our resilience will be tested in relationships, on our job, with our finances, and with our health. When we rely on our faith in God, our resilience starts to kick in. allowing us to become stronger with time and overcome the adversities that we will face. I believe, as I said before, that it starts when we are young. There are times that we must make sacrifices of not getting everything we want and when we want it. Including doing things we don't want to do but having the mindset of persevering through life's experiencing when it doesn't feel good. We may not see the plan during the process, but I assure you that pressing through will make a better you and a better me. Stretch high, Stretch wide, Stretch big, Stretch far. Don't stop, keeping stretching.

14.2 - OBSTACLES IN THE MOMENTS OF PROGRESS

Throughout our life, we will always run into obstacles, but we can't let them stop us. Majority of my life, besides raising my kids, I worked on a job in the hospitality industry, which was most known for as the hotel business. I would say that it is a very good industry to be in, especially for young, motivated, skilled, and professional individuals with a great personality and who like working around people and are self-motivated about delivering great service. There is money to be made, and overtime is welcomed. If you don't have major responsibilities outside of work, working in the industry can surely accommodate your lifestyle. It was definitely a great career to have when I first started before the year 1997. I had no idea that this was the path God was choosing for me. "I didn't choose it, but it chose me!" I don't regret it one moment. I made good money, I met great people, not just the guests that I was serving but I felt like the people I worked with were my family away from home. I enjoyed the special service and respect that we would give one another which allowed me the opportunity to set my standards high on what service is really is about. It was the standard of calling the guest by their last names. It was an environment where everybody knew your name, even the guest. The industry is about having a listening ear and showing compassion for others. Have you ever had someone you not familiar with to call you by your name? Have you ever had someone go out of their way to try to please you or accommodate you? Do you not feel special? If you have never felt this type of treatment, try it out on someone else, and eventually, you will reap the results back in return. Your return may not be with the person that you served. It may be someone else who you don't expect. My motto is, "You don't have to look for what you can get back in return when you provide good service because the blessings will follow you." One of the most powerful ways of serving is when we accommodate someone else rather than ourselves. This is what my career has been about for over 20 years, and I have loved every minute of it. I have experienced that there are people that seems as if they have it really going on has issues and problems too. Some of us just like to paint a perfect picture about others, but if we gaze at the art of the picture and look closely, we can then focus on the realistic images. We will then take notice that there is art that has been painted for how people want you to perceive them or how you paint your own picture of others. You will begin to discern that money does not bring us permanent joy. You will begin to realize that people do not bring us peace. You will begin to not expect others to give Love when you don't have it yourself. It's not our responsibility to find Love, but it's our responsibility to give it. Why? Every single human being long for it. It's in our nature to desire it. It's what keeps life going. Therefore, it's our obligation to show it. Once we show it, we can expect it! We are such selfish creatures that we want to receive it first before being willing to show it. Back to the story and making my point. It wasn't always smooth, loving, and happy sailing on my job. It was during the encounters of my obstacles at the job that I had the opportunity to see God our Father at his best. I had so many different challenges, from bad spirits, unfairness, and just very low morale in the workforce. I felt like those challenges were the obstacles that were hindering me from being the person I wanted to be. Oh No! The complete opposite. The obstacles that seem to have been in my life only molded me to trust in God more. Love people more and helped me to change my character, all while learning God's character. Throughout my career, there were so many obstacles that tried to keep me from being where God was trying to get me. I'm sure most can relate to leaders holding you back or seeing you as a person that is not capable of reaching your highest potential. Experiencing unfairness. Not holding others accountable for their laziness which causes others to take up the slack. I felt like I was good enough to train an employee to do the job, but I was not good enough to take on a greater role. A couple of leaders constantly tried to find ways to get me out the door because I was speaking up for what I believed. But God... He's Bigger! Those that tried to get rid of me failed in their attempt. In exchange, they were removed from my life. That is why it is so important to let God fight our battles. You will go through something, but he will make certain that your situation will turn out fair in the end. God will give us peace during the moment of our storms, he will rescue us from our enemies and anything that wants to cause us harm. Obstacles will find you and when it cross your path, we will have to use the most powerful weapons. God's words.

Steps to take when we go against our enemy

*Pray to the Heavenly Father with a specific request.

*Trust in God patiently, expecting that he will come through in his way and his timing

*Quote one of the most powerful scriptures "No weapons formed against me, will prosper." Isaiah 54:17

Giving your obstacles to the Heavenly Father eliminates the stress and won't allow our energy to fall into the hands of the enemy. Our enemy will do everything within its harmful power to keep us from trusting God, fulfilling his purpose, and living out our destiny.

Lesson to be learned:

Obstacles will cross our path, but we must rely on prayer and quoting God's powerful scriptures to remove the evil attacks that try to steal, kill, and destroy our destiny.

CHAPTER 15 –LIVING YOUR PURPOSE

15.1 - AN INTENTIONAL CREATOR

The only way we will find genuine joy and fulfillment in the life of our career is by discovering our unique talents and spiritual gifts through glorifying our Heavenly Father. We are not on earth to build an everlasting home. We are on earth to work towards living in God's Holy Kingdom. We as believers should have the standards to worship God only, submit to him faithfully, and strive to do his will and not our own. Our lives are never meaningless because living for the Lord is the greatest purpose we can have. Our Heavenly Father wants us to serve our purpose with humbleness, kindness and Love. Without these merits, the value of our purpose will be worthless. Our Father is an intentional creator who never fails at what he does. He does things on purpose, deliberately and calculated. His words contain a wealth of instructions for building a righteous and meaningful life. A life that's full of value and purpose. Our responsibility is to learn the facts about our father and pursue having a personal relationship with him. Our assignments are to meditate on his promises, follow his guidance, and obey his instructions. We are held accountable when we are not asking for our purpose in life. We may look for fame, riches, and the pleasures of the world, but will it sustain us when the world has failed us? Because the world will fail us. People will fail us because we are human beings born into this world of imperfection. The world is assembled with many disappointments. Through our self-centered plans, it sometimes causes us to be derailed from our itinerary, but nothing can alter our Heavenly Father's plans and the purpose he has in place. My prayer is that we welcome Jesus Christ to come into our hearts and remain there. Greet the Holy Spirit with kindness as he empowers us to be employees for the Lord. Remain faithful to God, and he will place you into your right position and carry you through your life's journey.

Actions

15.2 - J.O.B. SECURITY

15.3 - JESUS OPPORTUNITY BENEFITS

Our job security is not based on man but our Heavenly Father. Why? Because God is our security. He has the final say. He owns everything. If we live in fear, we close the doors to a potential opportunity. When we choose to stay closed-minded, we miss out on the chance of experiencing something more than what we are used to. When we focus on our limitations, it causes us to doubt our abilities which interferes with how we think of ourselves and what we believe about ourselves. When our security has been compromised with our fear, we will not reap the full benefits that come with great possibilities. Looking at it from the opposite angle. Instead of pursuing our salary, we may have to downsize our wages in order to be placed on the payroll of fulfillment. When our security is being trusted in the Lord, we can make an executive decision of stepping out in faith with a different mindset of guidelines and a secure assurance of Godly principles.

* Stay focus-on the word and his promises

* Keep trusting-looking beyond what we see to what God sees

* Love patiently-when you don't understand the process

* Pray without ceasing, prayer changes things

Scriptures to Secure your Benefits:

(1John 4:18)

"There is no fear in Love, and Perfect Love casts out fear. For fear has to do with punishment, and whoever fears has not been perfected in Love."

(Proverbs 3:5-6), "Trust in the Lord with all thy heart, lean not unto our own understanding. In all thine ways, acknowledge him, and he will direct your path."

(John 10:10), (John 14:6), Jesus said, "I come that you may have life and have it more abundantly" "I am the way, truth, and life, no man cometh unto the Father except through me." Will you secure your life today as Jesus becomes your savior?

(John 3:16), "God so loved the world that he gave his only son, and whosoever will believe in his son will not perish but have eternal life."

(Jeremiah 29:11), "I know the plans I have for you, declare the Lord, plans to prosper you and not to harm you. Plans to give you hope and a future."

(Proverbs 11:28), "those who trust in themselves are fools, but those who walk in wisdom are kept safe."

(Romans 15:13),"Fill your hope with joy and peace as you trust in God, that you may overflow with hope by the power of the Holy Spirit."

(Joshua 1:9), "Be strong and courageous. Do not be afraid, nor discouraged, for the Lord our God is with us wherever you go."

(Psalms 56:4)," I will put my trust in God; I will not be afraid. I will not fear what man of the flesh can do to me."

(Ephesians 4:2), "With all humility and gentleness seek patience, standing with one another in Love."

(Matthew 21:22), "In all things whatsoever we ask in prayer and believing, we shall receive."

(Romans 8:28), "All things work together for the good of those that love God and to those that are called according to his purpose."

401K Plan

(Galatians 6:9), "Let's not grow weary of doing good, for, in due season, you will reap a harvest if we don't give up."

(Deuteronomy 8:18), "We should remember the Lord our God, for it is he that gives us the power to gain wealth."

(Proverbs 3:9), "Honor the Lord with your wealth and with the first fruits of all your increase."

(Luke 6:38), "Give, and it shall be given to you."

(Malachi 3:10), "Bring the whole tithe into the storehouse that there may be food in the house. Test me says the Lord and see if I will open the floodgates of heaven and pour out so much blessing that there will not be room enough to store it."

(Proverbs 10:22), "The blessings of the Lord make a person rich, and he adds no sorrow with it."

(Jeremiah 17:7-8), "Blessed are those who trust in the Lord and have made the Lord their hope and confidence." We are like trees planted along a riverbank with roots that reach deep into the water. These trees are not bothered by the heat or worried about the drought, and the leaves manage to stay green and never stop bearing their fruit.

(2 Corinthians 9:8), "God will generously provide all you need. Then you will always have everything you need and plenty left to share with others."

(Philippians 4:19), "God will supply all of your needs according to his riches in glory by Christ Jesus." What he does for one, he will do for others also.

MASTER YOUR CRAFT BY CREATING YOUR LEGACY

A simple definition for mastering your craft is the ability to do something with great skill and sticking with the process of learning new ways of making your craft better. A simple definition for legacy is the accomplishments of an individual's life that make a great impact on others. Just to name a few of my own personal individuals who have impacted my life in different ways. Rev. Dr. Martin Luther King Jr. was a well-known civil rights activist and leader. He left his legacy, amongst other things, to **"Choose Love over Hate"**. Chadwick Bozeman, actor, and entertainer left his legacy by inspiring others to **"Never give up on their dreams, and through obstacles and circumstances, you can achieve your goals through perseverance and courage"**. Michael Jackson, singer, and entertainer. He left his legacy with us through his passion for music, and now we can listen to his craft from all generations to come. Jesus, the son of the living God. He left his legacy by coming on the earth to save us from sin by offering free salvation because of His Love for us. Lastly but certain not least, my parents. They left their legacy by laying down a foundation of having faith in God. They taught me the values and the significance of becoming a lady with a heart of service and having a loving heart through my actions. The process of mastering your craft starts with the heart. I'm certain I can speak from a human being perspective that we all want to be good at something. The difference is that some of us only talk about wanting to do better. There are others that don't give it a thought, and there are those that take the necessary steps to get better. When we master our craft by loving what we do and setting out a purpose for doing it. It will ultimately lead us into success. What is success? Success is mainly an accomplishment of what we aim for in order to complete a personal purpose. Therefore, success does not define us, but we define what success is in our life. We should not only desire to accomplish something by being successful, but we should equally desire to leave a legacy that will impact others. It starts with our own personal fulfillment. Fulfillment is a delightful feeling that when something we desire has been achieved it will bring joy, satisfaction, and peace to our inner being. I would imagine that everyone wants some sort of fulfillment. Fulfillment is sprouted within. Launching Love as your career will allow mastering your craft to create your own uniqueness. We just have to evaluate ourselves and tap into what makes us interesting individuals by getting creative, skilled, and doing it with heart.

Having a purpose is essential. Without purpose and passion for something, it makes it difficult to pursue something and persevere while doing it. Many of us use the term setting goals, but does it line up with part of mastering your craft? I would rather use the phrase setting your purpose. We often time set goals but are they the goals that are meant for us. Setting your purpose allows us to be able to follow through and achieve the task. Anything that is worth having is more suitable to pursue.

Oftentimes we are on social media or looking at someone else's life when we should take time to discover who we are and get to know ourselves. Without taking steps to connect with our creator and grow into a meaningful relationship with him, it's difficult to find our true calling. We may master a skill that brings us wealth, but will we leave this earth with a legacy that follows joy, peace, satisfaction and fulfillment to ourselves while impacting others with a loving heart.

Keynote: Instead of setting goals, focus on setting your purpose.

"Love"

Love is special, Love is kind

Love is a relationship that intertwines.

Love can sometimes be tough, Love can sometimes bring pain

But Love is a wonderful feeling to gain.

Love is not just a word that we speak, Love shows actions

Which makes it unique.

Love you cannot buy, but Love you can certainly give

O what an awesome way to let love live!

Love demonstrates many attributes, that you dare not miss out

Because Love is our purpose and that's what this entire book is all   about.

Let's not waste time by not showing our Love,

So that we won't suffer the consequences of being separated from the creator who's up above.

Romans 8:39

By: Angel Little

ABOUT AUTHOR

My first book "Launching Love as Your Career" has taken me to another level of success. I'm a mother of two biological sons and one stepson. I've been in the hospitality industry for over 25 years. After completing high school, I pursued the career of becoming a fashion designer at the Art Institute of Atlanta. However, 2 years later, I discovered that becoming a fashion designer wasn't what I thought it would be and that's when I started my career at Ritz Carlton Hotel, Downtown Atlanta. God had chosen another route for me. I didn't know it at the time, but I realized it as I drew closer to God. He eventually showed me what my purpose was and I'm super excited to find out where he continues to take me in the future. As for now, I'm just enjoying the journey.

Made in the USA
Columbia, SC
07 February 2022

55615643R00085